The
Golden Dawn

Professor Hilton Hotema

ISBN: 978-1-63923-123-2

The Golden Dawn

Table of Contents

Notice To All Concerned

Be it known all men by these presents that statements contained in this volume are based on facts observed and facts inferred, the known laws of Creation, the statements of the Bible, and other ancient scriptures as they are and have beeen interpreted.

No claim is made intentionally as to what any method cited may do for any one in any case, and it is recognized and understood that the author and publisher of this work assume no responsibility for any opinion presented or expressed, nor the results that may occur in any case wherein any one may decide to pursue any path mentioned in this work.

The author of this work is not available for engagements, receives no visitors, grants no interviews, and has no desire to become Exhibit A for curiosity seekers. He has no message for the public except those contained in his writings, and he discusses with no one the matters about which he writes.

The publisher of this work has no authority to give any one the address of the author, nor to comment upon the opinions expressed or the postulates presented in these writings. His engagement is to publish and sell the work, and there his obligation ends.

Professor Hilton Hotema
Honolulu, 1967

Special Notice

This work is prepared and published for the benefit and enlightenment of mankind, and permission is hereby granted to quote from it, provided full credit is given to author and publisher.

The Publisher

The Golden Dawn

After long age of deception under the rule of the Mother Church, *the Golden Dawn* is sharply gleaming on the distant horizon, denoting the arrival of a brighter day in the life of Man, the Lord of the whole earth, according to the Bible *(Zechariah 4:14)*

The Mother Church, born in darkness, developed in the blood of millions of innocent victims who refused to embrace its false dogma, sustained by instilling the fear of death into the mind of the masses, beholds the brilliant reflection of *the Golden Dawn* and trembles.

For the sign of the apprcach of the Golden Dawn heralds the revival of the lost Wisdom of the Ancient Magi; which informs man of the mysteries of Creation that will liberate his mind from the fear of death.

The lost Wisdom taught man that he is life, and that life had no beginning and has no ending. The condition called death pertains only to the body and not to life. And the body was never alive. It was only the mechanism used by life to perform its regular duties in the visible world according to the laws of Creation

THERE IS NO DEATH. The condition called death is the regular creative process that releases the Eternal Ego from its earthly prison. This process is a change that is not understood by man, due to false teaching of the Church, designed to keep man in darkness and ignorance. The Apostle Paul clearly expounded this baffling secret in these words:

"Behold, I show you a mystery: We shall not sleep (in death), but we shall all be changed, in a moment, in the twinkling of an eye, at the last trump" *(1 Corinthians 15:51, 52)*.

What Paul called change is the liberation of the Divine Ego from its earthly prision, so it can return to its heavenly home. And so Death, when correctly understood, is a blessing, not a curse, and was so regarded by the Ancient Magi.

The gnostic poet Phocylides declared that, "After we have left our earthly prision we shall be gods, for in us dwell immortal and incorruptible souls."

A tomb inscription at Petilia, in Italy, which dates back to fourth Century B.C. said; "It is a glorious mystery which comes to us from the blessed gods; for us mortals, death is not an evil but a good."

Theognia asserted: "Life in the flesh is but deception and misery."

Sopholes stated: "The first good thing is to be born, and the second is to die as soon as possible."

The ancient philosopher Cleombrotus, of Ambracia, threw himself from a tower, that with a single leap he might return to his heavenly home.

Hegesias of Cyrene, surnamed Perisithanates (he who advocates death as a blessing)., made a business of teaching that Death is far better than life. His disciples killed themselves in such numbers that Ptolemy Philadelphus closed his school and banned him from traching in Alexandria.

The gospel Jesus said: "It is the Spirit that quickeneth: the flesh profiteth nothing" *(John 6:63)*.

But the Mother Church changed all that ancient philosophy, and invented and substituted its dogma to the effect that unless we embraced the gospel Jesus as our Savior, we would go to hell when we died and burn and suffer forever in "a lake of fire burning with brim-stone" *(Revelation 19:20, 20:10)*.

That was the terrible teaching we heard eighty years ago when we went to church and Sunday-school. But that line of teaching has been greatly change since then, due to the light of knowledge that heralds the coming of *the Golden Dawn*.

Chapter No. 1
Priests

In tracing the priesthood from its origin to its present sphere, we must constantly keep in mind two dominating factors: First, the prisesthood originated with, and developed under, the worship of mythical gods which represented the power and agencies of creation, as shown by the records of the ancient world: hence, priestcraft is founded entirely upon fiction. And second, the motive impelling its orign and development was, and will always be, selfishness and mercenary, and its guiding star, gain and greed for these men are only human as all other men.

Early man had no priests. They came with the development of man's social character, and originally man had no society. The primal step in that direction came with the family. The father was its head. He protected it, provided for it, and logically ruled it. To his family, he was a superman. He had no religion, he worshipped no god, and he obeyed no man.

In the course of time, several related families united into one big family, and this created the first tribe. With this unition, man's social character commenced. Conditions required the family heads to surrender some of their authority to the combination. Security required the tribe to be governed much as the single family had been. The shrewdest and strongerst, either by selection or seizure, took control and ruled. Man had begun to organize, but his organization was very crude. From this beginning, evolution created our modern society.

Then developed the faking parasites, and they found a gullible world. Here they were, the necromancer, the diviner, the sorcerer, the soothsayer, the medicine man, the conjurer, the spiritual medium, the wizard, the fortune teller, the seer, and last but most contemptible, the prophet and the priest.

Foresseing the rich rewards to be gained, many of the shrewdest fakers became priests. And the early rulers of all nations have been the priests, generally, the High Priest was king. He taxed the people, and built the temples for the priests and other religions parasites. The kings resided in the temples. The people had little or nothing to do with the temples, except to feed, clothe, and keep the priest-king in luxury.

To perpetuate their status, the priests created a caste system, with themselves as the ruling-privileged class. India is still cursed with the system. And its infulence is reflected in all countries thru the religious, financial and social standing of the people.

These priest-kings of old built thousands of massive temples in which to live and worship their mythical gods. To do so, they filched enormous treasures from the people. In the city of Pagan, on the Irrawaddy River in Burma, there are nearly ten thousand of these ancient temples. Such temples are scattered all over the ancient world.

All the gods were myths; all of the millions of priests officiating were charlatans and imposters, and all of the millions of worshippers were deceived and defrauded. For thousands of years this robbery and deception continued. The ignorant, deluded people lived in mud huts, labored, bled and died that they could construct these monster edifices to their mythical gods — gods portrayed to them by the priests.

For centuries Egypt was a priest governed, priest cursed country. The pharaohs were the High priests, the sons of Gods. For more than two thousand years, the Egyptian priests rolled in wealth and luxury, at the people's expense. They built pyramids, temples and sacred structures with slave labor. The people were their slaves, and feared them as none but the ignorant can fear.

By the beginning of the 14th Century B. C., the situation was appalling. A new ruler rose to power, Amenhotep IV. He understood the priest- ridden situation of his people, and set out to alleviate it . He broke with the priests, and closed all their temples. He sought to put an end to all sectarian rites, prohibiting the worship of all gods by Aton, the sun's disk. He changed his name to Akhenaton, the sun's glory, and moved his capital to Tell–el–Amarna, as there were too many priests in Thebes to suit him. He knew he was not the son of any god, and said so. He refused to be a charlatan and deceive his people. Truly, a rare ruler.

But he was a sickly man, and his reign was short. It was only twelve years, and not enough priests had died. There were too many living when he died, and they had opposed him in every possible way they could. At his death, the priests gathered like vultures and gained control of the feeble Smenkhare, successor of Akhenaton. They settled down upon the people's fleshpots, they ruled again, and exacted their tithes. All their old gods were resurrected, and the people were forced to feed and support the priests.

Think of the billions of gullible people these priests deceive. Think of the billions of wealth and millions of lives sacrificed in the construction of the massive temples.

In the Philippines nearly seventy years ago , when we were there as a U. S. soldier shooting our way thru the

Insurrection, we were surprised to see a fine stone Catholic Church in little villages, surrounded by palmetto and bamboo huts where the natives lived, and most of the churches were equipped with pipe organs.

As the Catholics did not control us then, we usually quartered in the churches, as they were about the only fit places for us to live and sleep; and the soldiers who could play the organ had lots of enjoyment playing those pipe organs. Had our officers been Catholic, they would not have allowed that.

The modern priests are following the path of the old, and all are doing a thriving business. They glean annually from their dupes in this country more than a billion dollars, and in one way or another they control all the various departments of federal, state, country and municipal governments. They have succeeded in doing this in the Christian World for sixteen hundred years.

But all signs indicate the tide is turning. The people are not quite so gullible and ignorant as of old, and the good work of science is bringing Light and eliminating the gods of old. If this encouraging progress continues, the modern temples will become schools, the gods will be deserted, and the priests will become useful teachers.

Chapter No. 2
The Priestly Fable

"And ye shall be unto me a kingdom of Priests, and an holy nation. These are the words which thou shalt speak unto the children of Israel. And Moses came and called for the elders of the people, and laid before their faces all the words which the Lord commanded him. And all the people answered together, and said, All that the Lord hath spoken we will do. And Moses returned the words of the people unto the Lord" *(Exodus 19:6-8).*

Moses appeared to be on very close terms with the Lord. Who wrote that statement? Not Moses, for he appears in the third person. It was another one of those fabulous statements, many of which run all thru the Bible, written by the priests for the benefit of the priests.

And that leads directly to Bibliolatry, a condition invented and taught by the church, — a blind, forced, unfounded, superstitious belief in the Bible literally, based not on bold facts but on fraudulent claims of the church, that every word in the Bible is a direct revelation of its God.

The gullible memebers and followers of Christianity, who exalt the Bible above all other books as the "Word of God", have not studied it and do not know what it contains. Usually they have not even read more than a chapter here and a passage there. No other book is more reverenced and less known than this so-called "Book of Holy Writ."

Ignorance of the contents of the Bible is indispensable to faith in the book. And it is this ignorant veneration that makes it dangerous for a thinking person to reveal the facts behind the Bible's compilation.

During the thousand years that the Church possessed and exercised its great power, those who studied the Bible or questioned its "holy authenticity" were either hacked to pieces or burned to death. Even now, challengers are persecuted as much as public opinion and the law will allow.

In 1926 M. M. Mangasarian wrote: "It's a matter of history that in the name of this Jewish-Christian volume, which people do not read and are but superficially acquainted with, nearly a hundred million lives in Europe alone have been destroyed by the Church" *(The Neglected Book, page 14)*.

Before the 19th Century, if a person publicly questioned any statement in the Bible, or attempted to investigate the background there of and state his findings, he was risking his very life.

With the beginning of the 19th Century, the great power which the Church had ruthlessly wielded for a thousand years, declined to where it was safer for a person to let it be known that he did not believe the Bible according to the letter of the word. The result of this has been that an enormous amount of amazing light has been thrown on the Bible by the work of unprejudiced researchers, and some surprising facts have been revealed.

Until the 19th Century the hieroglyphics of Egypt and the cuneiform inscriptions of Babylonia and Assyria were undecipherable and their messages not understood. And so the Bible was our sole authority for ancient history prior to the rise of Greek civilization.

With the discoveries by archeologists of the key to the hieroglyphics and cuneiform inscriptions, there has been revealed the existence of highly developed civilizations long before the time previously assigned, on the authority of the biblical genealogies.

Also, the Egyptian and Assyrian monuments made it possible to reconstruct with a great degree of accuracy, the history of the ancient civilizations during the period to which the Bible relates, and much of it fails to agree with the biblical statements.

While there are points of agreement between the biblical record and the ancient monuments, there are many important points where the messages cut in stone not only fail to confirm the biblical records, but flatly refute them.

And so the Bible, as the word of God, shows that God did not tell the story according to the messages of the ancient people which they carved in their stone monuments.

Widely scattered thru ancient and modern volumes may be found most of what we say in this work. Many able authors have shown the so-called Sacred Scriptures to be unhistorical, and pronounced them largely legendary, spurious, and even fradulent.

Beyond the arrangement of this work, little is claimed as original. Ideas, phrases, and even whole paragraphs have been lifted from the writings of others, and, in most cases, acknowledged.

The most amazing feature of the whole matter perhaps, is the fradulent manner in which the pious Church fathers made their Holy Bible, and the gullibility of the deceived masses in swallowing the priestly fraud as the Word of God.

The credulous masses don't know that after the founding of the church in the 4th Century, an army of trusted, prejudiced scribles went to work, and worked under the watchful eye of the church.

A huge task confronted them. Thousands of scrolls in the Alexandrian Library had to be examined, and some selected for use in making the bible. And others to be used to compile a fraudulent history of the ancient world.

For the church had to make ancient history agree with its claims that the ancient pagans were an ignorant, superstitious, heathenish people, and the Christian Church was born to save the world and to lead humanity from the darkness of ignorance into the light of knowledge.

This fraudulent work of the church Fathers in compiling the bible and revising ancient history to make it agree with the claims of the Church, is even admitted by certain statements in the Catholic Encyclopedia.

In volume 4, page 498, appears the statement that it was the custom of the (Church) scribes to lengthen out here and there, to harmonize passages, and to add their own explanatory material.

It also asserted that, "It is the public character of all (church) scribes to mold and bend the scared oracles until they comply with their own fancy, spreading them ... like a curtain, closing together, or drawing them back as they pleased."

In volume 7 page 645, it is stated that "Even the genuine Epistles were greatly interpolated to lend weight to the personal views of their authors."

And what could be more informing and enlightening as to the fraudulent work of the church Fathers than this frank statement in volume 12, page 768:

"There was need for a revision (of the ancient writings), which is not yet complete, ranging from all that has handed down from the Middle Ages."

Of this "revision" of anicent history, Godfrey Higgins stated:

"Every ancient author, without exception, has come down to us in this way thru the medium of christian editors, who have corrupted them all" *(The Anacalypsis)*.

And the great historian Gibbon, in his "Decline and fall of Rome," asserted that — "Eusebius, the greatest of the Christian historians, indirectly confessed that he had related whatever might redound to the glory of religion, and suppressed all that could tend to the disgrace of it."

All the declarations advanced by those writers who have charged the Church Fathers with committing fraud in their work and writings for the benefit and success of Christianity, are supported by the damaging acknowledgment of the Church Fathers themselves.

Chapter No. 3
Church

A church is a group of people banded together for religious worship.

Prior to the Christian era, there were few churches. Paganism was a religion of the priests, by the priests, and for the priests. Christianity is less so, but controlled by the same selfish motives.

The Christian world is more intelligent, more independent than were the worshippers of the pagan gods, and the priests act with more discretion.

The pagan priests ruled both the church and the state. The Christian priests did the same for many centuries, during the Dark Ages that lasted for a thousand years. While they still wield a dominating power over the submissive flocks of morons, they do it more gently, and with greater tact than of old. They mingle more with their subjects, stand less upon ceremony, and are more democratic than were the priests of Zeus or Osiris.

There is also a difference from anicent worship. The congregations take a greater part in church liturgies. Their environment is different too. There is not the stiffness in the construction of the modern temples. They are less massive, less costly, and more inviting. The cold, bleak walls are broken with attractive decorations, the great open rooms and chapels are filled with conveniences for the devout.

The ancient temples were different. They contained little, except monster figures of gods to impress the gullible people, such as winged bulls, serpents, and the altar upon which the sacrifices were made. These sacrifices were often members of the body politic or their children.

The Greek and Rome gods were in human form, but the ritual differed very little from the others. They sacrificed human beings, as did the Jews, Phoenicians and the others. The good divinities were importuned to be better, and the evil spirits begged to do less evil. The sacrifices were the god's pay for behaving, and the priests got their pay for their work.

The ceremonies of the Roman State Church are patterned after the pagan rites, but more refined. The priests do not sacrifice bulls, or men, or children, but carry scared relics, and life-sized figures of their god about the temples, less in human but equally ludicrous.

Attached to the pagan temples of old, were a whole retinue of priests, priestesses and servants, all supported and fed by the people.

To keep the people pouring their money in, they were occasionally called together and the fear of the gods and devils dinned into their ears, just as is done in the present time.

The modern cry, "Give unto the Lord" constantly reverberates in their ears. For this purpose the early priests made the people afraid of them and the priests have ever since followed that rule. By reason of this fear and hope of reward, the credulous people brought their savings to the priests, and presents for their gods. The people were taught the gods would be good to them if they were good to the gods and their priests, with emphasis on Priests — for they got it all.

During the Dark Ages the priests were the only writing class, the only reading class, the only learned and the only thinkers; they were all the professional class of that time.

Why did they for a thousand years possess all knowledge? The answer is to the everlasting shame of the Roman State Church.

Why did the priests not diffuse their learning amoung the masses, lift the veil of darkness from the people, and smooth their path to a brighter, happier life? They feared that would cause them to lose their monopoly and their power over the people.

The priesthood had no charity. They were just men, shrewd men, selfish men, unscrupulous men. They desired to live in luxury. Greed made their decision for them. They give up nothing. What did it matter if the poor and ignorant did remain poor and ignorant, did starve, go naked, and live in mud huts, so long as the vicars of the gods could reside in magnificent temples, wear gorgeous raiment, and live on the fat of the land.

Yes, the priests were the educated class, and they saw to it that they remained so. They had a monopoly, and were determined to maintain it. They would keep the common herd from becoming learned. They were easier scared and controlled. You cannot scare or control intelligence and the priests knew it.

The priests knew that learning and superstition would not mix. They knew learning would free mankind, and do exactly what it has done and is doing — but not doing it fast enough. It has already broken the shackles of the church, and partially released man from darkness. It was learning that drove the church out of government. It was learning that destroyed the cursed inquisition. It was learning that gave to us the privilege to write this, and prevent the Church from burning us at the iron stake for doing it.

Had they been honest men, the priests would have taught the young of their day and diffused learning. They would have picked up Ancient Civilization and carried it forward. Instead, they crushed learning that they might keep their greedy fingers in the flesh pots of humanity.

When the priests could no longer control learning, they tried to regulate it. They introduced Parochial Schools. Not free schools. *"Catch em young, they bend easier."* Regulate the schools where the child's thinking is done for him. If the youths must be educated, educate them the priest's way. Teach them nothing to conflict with the false doctrine of fear and superstition.

They must not know the facts relative to the history of their Bible, Church or God. Conceal that, and we can still retain our power.

What a glorious civilization would we have, had there been no blighting inquisition, and the Galileos, the Brunos, DeMolays, and countless other thinkers, been permitted to tell the slaves of the church that the world is round; that it revolves about the sun; that disease is not the work of devils; that there were no such monsters as witches, unicorns, dragons, cockatrices, or the other monsters presented in the Christian Bible and vouched for by the priesthood.

There have been more than one priesthood. Each nation has been cursed with one. Egypt, Syria, Babylon — yes, they all had a different tribe of the parasites, and then, as now, each held its gods were the only true gods, and the others imposters and frauds.

We know now, they were all myths, and the priests imposters. The priests knew it then.

If there were a true god, why did't he consolidate the people under the true faith? He could not expect the priests to; their jealousy and intolerance would prevent it. No, the priests of each nation were in the saddle, and did not propose to be unhorsed.

It was the priests greedy lust for power and wealth that ultimately set man free. It was the priest's peddling indulgences, giving man the right for a price, to kill his neighbor without sin, that caused the Church revolt. That produced Luther, Zwingli, Calvin, and other reformers. These men divided the priest craft, and then began fighting among themselves. While they were engaged in this foghting, man broke the shackles of intolerance and escaped.

As the superstition of the Dark Ages fades out and the glorious light of knowledge floods the Christian world, the Golden Dawn of a New Age sharply gleams on the distant horizon. As the Golden Dawn advances, the Mother Church retreats.

Surprising evidence of this gloomy retreat appears in the Gallup Poll published in the press of April 12, 1967. The report said:

"The current thesis that the Church is losing its relevance in today's world gains support from the results of the latest Gallup survey."

That report showed that 57% of the people of this country assert that religion is losing its influence on American life. Ten years ago the proportion holding this view was only 14%. If that rate continues for another decade, the churches will be almost empty.

The younger generation, born and living in a world of more light, is the group that is falling the fastest from the world of religion. The above report said:

"Declining church attendance of the nation's younger people, those in their 20's accounts for most of this loss."

One publication asserted that the "greatest of all menaces to the churches is the 'God Is Dead' movement, led by some important clergymen who advance the idea that 'you can be a Christian and an atheist'" (Reverend Ernest Harrison, in *A Church Without God*).

The Mother Church, born in darkness, developed in the blood of millions of innocent victims, sustained by the fear of death, sees the approach of the Golden Dawn and trembles.

Chapter No. 4
The Inquisition

True history relates that in 1808 Napoleon decreed that the terrible Inquisition of the Mother Church in Spain, should be abolished.

Colonel Lemanowsky, representing Napoleon, called on Marshal Soul, then Governor of Madrid. The troops required for the undertaking were granted, and, as Commanding officer, Lemanowsky proceeded to the seat of the Inquisition, nearly five miles out of the city, and summoned the Jesuit Fathers to surrender to the Imperial Army and open the gates of the Inquisition. The building was surrounded by a wall of great strength, and defended by the soldiers of the "Holy Office."

Responding to a shot from the soldiers of the "Holy Office" which killed one of his men, Colonel Lemanowsky's troops opened fire, and after heroic efforts by the besiegers, the walls began to tremble, a breach was made, and the Inquisitor General appeared, followed by the Father Confessors, in their priestly robes, with long faces, and their arms crossed over their chests, their fingers resting upon their shoulders as if surprised at the disturbance, their assured complacency, indicating that the resistance was wholly unauthorized by them.

Their tricky artifice failed, and they were placed under guard, while their soldiers were secured as prisoners. "We then proceeded [says the account] to examine the stately edifice. We went from room to room and found all in good order. The apartments were richly furnished with altars, crucifixes and wax candles in abundance, but no evidence could be found of inquiry being practiced   none of the horrid features which we expected to find in an Inquisition.

"Splendid pictures adorned the walls. Beauty and splendor appeared everywhere — ceilings and floors of wood highly polished — marble floors — there was everything to please the eye and gratify a cultivated taste."

But where were those horrid instruments of torture reported to be there? And where those terrible dungeons in which human beings were said to be buried alive? The search for these seemed in vain, and the "Holy Fathers" gave "holy assurance" that they had been belied and that nothing had been concealed.

And so the visitors were about to retire. When Colonel Lemanowsky suggested that the marble floor be further examined. "Let water be brought and poured upon it," he said, "and we will watch and see if there is any place through which it passes more freely than others."

The "Holy Father" became disconcerted, and gave further "holy assurance" that nothing was concealed. But the officers with their swords and the soldiers with their bayonets, cleared out the suspicious seam through which the water had freely passed, while the "Holy Fathers" vainly remonstrated — when a soldier, by accident, hit with the butt of his gun a secret spring, and the marble slab raised up, revealing the secret stairway down which some of the soldiers descended, and such a horrible sight as met their eyes can hardly bear description. Solitary cells, where the victims of inquisitorial hate were confined year after year until death released them from their terrible suffering.

Some of the victims had been dead a long time, and only their bones remained chained to the wall of their cells. Men and Women, young and old, the sad victims of the "Mother Church."

In an adjoining room were instruments of torture of every description, ready to impose extreme agony upon their victims by means of various devices. The sight of these infernal engines of cruelty and torture kindled the fire of indignation in the bosom of the soldiers. They declared that every one of the Inquisitors should be put to the torture. They began with the Leader of the "Holy Fathers."

In spite of pleadings and resistance, the Inquisitors were compelled to meet the fate they had so freely and willingly decreed for their victims.

Colonel Lemanowsky wrote: "Having witnessed the torture of four of the barbarous Inquisitors, I left the soldiers to wreak their vengeance on the other   guilty inmates of that prison of hell.

"News spread rapidly to Madrid and multitudes rushed to that fatal spot. Such a meeting there was! It was like a resurrection! About 150 who had been buried for years were still alive, and fathers found their long lost daughters, wives were restored to their husbands, and parents to their children. "Later, when library, painting, furniture and other articles of value were removed, I sent for a wagon load of powder, and in a few moments the walls and turrets of the massive structure rose majestically in the air, impelled by a tremendous explosion, and then and there fell back to the earth an immense heap of ruins! The Roman Catholic Inquisition of Spain was no more." *(Behind Closed Doors, 1930)*.

And there you have a true historical account, and "holy" picture, of the "holy" doings of the "holy" Roman Catholic Church! In the words of ex-Priest Charles Chiniquy, "ROME

A PERMANENT POLITICAL CONSPIRACY UNDER THE MASK OF RELIGION."

Chiniquy was priest for 25 years. He had to leave because of the ever increasing corruption within this church (3000 of his people left with him!). He wrote one of the greatest exposures of Romanism ever published — *"Fifty Years In The Church of Rome."* In this book he devotes several pages to the MURDER OF ABRAHAM LINCOLN by Rome!

The "Church" would have us forget all this Inhuman, Ungodly, Insane Hellishness and put a Catholic at the head of our nation! Forget that upwards of A HUNDRED MILLION SLAUGHTERED (AND ROASTED ALIVE) "Heretics" in Her diabolical priestly scheme to FORCE Her copied (STOLEN) Religion upon and enslave the masses of all Earth.

All of these, each one of these murdered, to whom was given, by the Almighty Universal Law of the Cosmos, the same rights, privileges, liberties to Do, to THINK, to WRITE, to WORSHIP, as their own conscience dictated! This mighty Law employs a means of Retribution, which ALWAYS WORKS! It works for Evil or for Good! It never fails! It works with the individual; it works with groups; Church or otherwise! one of Her own priests stated; "The atonement of the Church draws near; She will go down in a night of blood."

This "holy" Church copied the material for the Bible from these ancient astrological scrolls. Her "holy" Church Fathers trans-literalized, mutilated and substituted (human characters in place of the astrological symbolisms). It took the compilers 80 years to complete the work, and when done it resembled the original no more than an elephant resembles a flea!

Please, Sleepy, Brain washed, so-called "Protestants," add to the above the following CHURCH LAWS of ROME.

Pope Leo XIII (Encyclical, Human Liberty, 1888): "It is quite unlawful to demand, or to grant unconditional FREEDOM OF THOUGHT, OF SPEECH, OF WRITING, OR OF WORSHIP." And a later one from Pius XII (April 6, 1951): "INDIVIDUAL LIBERTY IN REALITY IS A DEADLY ANARCHY." Then, from Catholic Encyclical Volume XIV, page 768, we have: "Heretics may be not only excommunicated (greatest blessing that can befall anyone!), BUT JUSTLY PUT TO DEATH."

Oh No! The "holy" Catholic Church doesn't want all this brought to light, just yet! It is not only traitorously Un-American, and opposed to everything for which our Great Constitution stands, but is Inhuman, Insane SLAVERY of the worst kind! And all THINKING Catholics should rise up against such Ungodly INTRIGUE! Such an Institution have an atom of "salvation" to offer? Just how stupid CAN humans become? Oh, this is but a "bubble". Here is some more:

From *Brownson's Quarterly Review,* another popish organ: "PROTESTANTISM OF EVERY FORM HAS NOT, AND NEVER CAN HAVE, ANY RIGHTS WHERE CATHOLICITY IS TRIUMPHANT." — Then to quote Priest Harney of New Brunswick, N.J., May. 7.1901: "Certainly the church does consider Protestants heretics — I do not doubt, IF THEY WERE STRONG ENOUGH, THAT THE CATHOLIC PEOPLE WOULD HINDER, EVEN BY DEATH, THE SPREAD OF SUCH ERRORS."

The Catholic aspirant for office falsely claims his religion will make no difference in the discharge of official duties. Oh, yes? Any "good" Catholic knows his allegiance is first to the pope. The Vatican being a Political State (NOTHING ELSE), this at once constitutes an act of TREASON against the U.S. Government! And now may we quote from a book by Shoups, used, we understand, in Roman Catholic schools and approved by Cardinal Manning: "The civil Laws are binding on the conscience ONLY SO LONG AS THEY ARE CONFORMABLE TO THE CATHOLIC CHURCH."

We could go on and on and quote many more. Isn't this plenty? Or does a whole stone building need to fall upon us before we awaken to the fact that this nation is on its way to Rome, Rum and RUIN!

Back to the Inquisition a moment: A single example of the horrible Slaughter — The Catholic Massacre of St. Bartholomew! Within three days' time from 60,000 to 75,000 Men, Women and Children were BUTCHERED! The streets ran red with blood! Priests were in the midst urging the hirelings on with promises of "Heavenly Rewards!" On this occasion the Pope had a MEDAL STRUCK IN HONOR OF THE AFFAIR!

Has there ever been any remorse manifested over this terrible inhuman slaughter by the "holy," "holy" Church of Rome? For answer we quote "Daddy" (Priest) Phelan, Editor of Western watchman, of November 21, 1921: "We have never written a line in extenuation or palliation of the Inquisition. We never thought it needed defense." WHAT MORE DO YOU NEED? However, we will yet quote more from this TRAITOR to the USA.

"Tell us we are Catholics first and Americans or Englishmen afterwards; of course we are — Why, if the government of the United States were at war with Church, we would say, TO HELL WITH THE GOVERNMENT OF THE UNITED STATES — WE WOULD SAY TO HELL WITH

ALL THE GOVERNMENTS OF THE WORLD — The pope is ruler of the world —" (June, 1913). Personally, this writer would be so ashamed to again belong to such a Gang of BUTCHERERS and DARE to entertain the thought that he was a "Child of God" — Well, suppose that YOU DO some THINKING instead of allowing a Lying Clergy do it for you?

General Lafayette said: "If the liberties of the American people are ever destroyed, they will fall by the hands of the Catholic clergy." Another French Author, *Emile Zola*, said: *"Civilization will not attain to its perfection until the last stone of the last church falls on the last priest."* ROMAN CHRISTIANITY is the GREATEST FRAUD ON EARTH TODAY!

George Washington said: "The government of the United States is in no sense founded upon the Christian religion."

Catholic influence at work today is attempting to attempt to instill the belief in the minds of the people that Catholic influence was behind the Founders of the nation! Fifty of the Fifty-six signers of the Declaration of Independence were Masons! They say, "Lie," in spite of an oath on the Bible; "BE UNTRUTHFUL FOR THE SAKE OF GOD IF IT WILL SAVE YOUR BODY FROM PUNISHMENT, AND YOUR SOUL FROM HELL." So? "Hell" a scheming INVENTION of the Church to SCARE poor dupes into GIVING to support this "PERMANENT POLITICAL CONSPIRACY UNDER THE MASK OF RELIGION." And help build more impressive TAX-FREE edifices.

Chapter No. 5
New Epoch

The first half of the 16th Century saw the light of a New Epoch spreading over Europe.

For more than a centuary, Moorish culture and learning had been battering at the church gates of ignorance and superstition. The power of the priests behind the gates was weakening. Intelligence and knowledge were breaking through.

Magellan, with the aid of the compass, that "instrument of the Devil" had sailed around the world, proving that the "Bible's Divine Truth" as to the earth was a sanctimonious lie. And the invention of printing had wrecked the divine right of the church to control learning. No longer could the forging scribes of the church insert in their copies of divine manuscripts whatever the church wanted, and get away with it.

And then books, in mass production, began to roll off the presses in spite of the interdicts of the church. Secret printing presses sprang up all over Europe, particularly in the great region of Germany, where Martin Luther had nailed his damning theses to the church door.

Printed matter flowed too fast for the oppenents of learning to control it. Men began to study that they night learn to read. No longer was all literature scared, to be read only by the priests. And in spite of the church, the sciences were being secretly revived and passed on to the people.

The Moors hed kept the spark of Greek and Roman culture burning, and the printing press fanned the flame into an unquenchable conflagration that even the Church's hellish

Inquisition could not extinguish. And further more, printing pried the strangling clutches of the priesthood loose from the throats of the states. And at last the church was slowely being relegated to control over mythical things only.

For twelve hundred years all literature and art in Europe had pertained strictly to religion. All the people had thought about, all they had talked about, and all they had dared to want to know, was "Christ and him crucified" *(1 Corinthians 2:3)*. Death by burning at the iron stake, or other fiendish punishment, was the penalty for doing otherwise.

Slowly and cautiously the people began to think and act differently. Then came Luther, Calvin, and a few others. Their work weakened the power of the Pope and started the flow of freedom. Yet, they were as intolerant with those who differed from them as was the church. But they had started something which even they could not stop.

No longer did thinking men blindly follow the text. "Set your affections on things above, not on things on the earth," nor believe they were "dead" and their lives "hid with Christ in God" *(Colossians 3:2, 3)*.

People began to think of the morrow, and how to make this a better world in which to live.

It's shocking to observe how the Church has trailed far behind the procession as learning and science have moved up the path of knowledge based on facts, not on fiction.

The church never changes a belief until ridicule or popular opinion forces it to do so. To the Church, the world was flat for fifty years after men had travelled entirely around it. To the priests, disease was caused by the devils that Christ drove into the hogs *(Matthew 8:28-34)*, long after science had proved otherwise. The Inquisition cut men into quarters for declaring the correct movements of the solar system, long after the fact had been established. The Church burned witches two centuries after they were known not to exist. The priests declared there were cockatrices, unicorns and other biblical monsters a century after Zoology proved they were mythical.

Slowly is the chrysalis of religious deception, and priestly chicanery cracking, and the true facts are slipping in.

The Church of England, that rock of salvation and aristocracy, that filching institution which still robs the poor by exacting the biblical one-tenth of all the poor's earnings, has been driven to admit that the conflicting biblical descriptions of Ceration are fiction, their belief the result of ignorance, and their story copied from mythology.

By the first half of the 16th Century, several efforts had been made to purge the clergy of vice. But like most crusades, they were only spasmodic. The clergy was generally immoral, and when the inevitable lull came after the crusading storm, the priests returned to their accustomed licentious pleasures.

Leo X succeeded Pope Julius, 1513, and the pot of church corruotion, stirred up by the reforming ladle of Luther, boiled over. The Pope was unable to read the signs. He refused to deviate from the ways of his predecessors. Hadn't the church always won over reformers? Of course, and it would again, he reasoned.

Rome continued its orgy of bacchanalian sin — the most vulgar of its performances being staged in the Vatican. As a reward for writing the most ribald comedies, the Pope appointed Bibbiena a Cardinal.

Leo was guilty of nepotism, simony, sodomy, lied in diplomacy, his agents peddled indulgences from town to town all over Europe; he confiscated the property of rich Cardinals, and had Cardinal Petrucci murdered for the same purpose. Such was his greed for luxury, vice, debauchery and dissipation, that he spent fifty million dollars in eight years, while Luther ranted about church iniquities.

The next two Popes, Adrian VI and Clement VII, were better men. They paddled around helplessly in the deep sea of Church filth, and were followed by Paul III (1534-1549). He was no better than the average run of Popes: but the Church revolt in Germany, England, and eleswhere, began to loom ominously, and Paul was forced to heed it. He hastily placed his relatives in lucrative offices, then called a meeting to reform the Church and quiet Luther.

A conference was help at Ratisbon, but it only tended to widen the Church breech. The conference did one thing, it awakened the Church from its slumbering debauchery to the real situation. To head off the heretics, it strengthened the cursed Inquisition throughout Europe, and particularly in Italy.

Loyal founded the "Society of Jesus," Jesuits to moralize the younger classes. The society was accepted by Pope Paul in 1540. It stove to educate the youth, but only church lines.

Had Pope Paul been sincere in his efforts to reform the Church the breech might have been remedied. But he did only what he was compelled to do; and once free from the clergy's immediate influence, he began to throw sand into the reform machinery.

He plotted a war to exterminate the Protestants. But it miscarried, and he was forced to call the council of Trent in 1545. This was to be a gathering of both orthodox and reformers, but the Pope, by bribing the bishops, manuevered it into a meeting to fix a set of rules that would strengthen his effort to exterminate the Protestants — ungodly heretics — he called them.

He death in 1549 was one of the most benign blessing that had come to the Church in 12 hundred years. While not the last of the vicious Popes, Paul's death marked the turning point in Church morals. Since then there has been a gradual improvement; moral betterment has kept pace with learnings, religious and political freedom.

At the beginning of the 16th Century, Rome had sunk to a filthy city of less tham 35,000 people; yet there were, relatively, 100 times as many murders and lesser crimes in Rome during that time, as there are in our American cities, yet, at the end of the century, there was a marked improvement in Rome's crime and vice.

The improvement has continued, and while the Church is still a most baneful influence on civilization, as shown by criminal records, the situation is not so bad as it was, because religion is slowly fading and losing its control of the masses due to the increase of knowedge based on true facts.

In the press of April 12, 1967 appeared a Gallup poll survey of the nation on this question:

"At the present time do you think religion as a whole is increasing its influence on American life, or losing its influence?"

The same poll was taken in 1957, and the response then showed that 14% of the people belived that religious influence was declining. In 1967, just a decade later, the response showed that 57% of the people believed that religious influence was declining in America.

At that alarming rate of increase, think what it will be in ten years from now. The report said:

"The shift in views on the influence of religion has been accompanied by a decline in the proportion of persons who attend church in a typical week — from 49% of the adult population who attended church in 1958 to 44% in 1966, — the low point to date."

This means that 56% of the adult population do not attend church in a typical week. It's encouraging to realize that people are waking up and are not the slaves of the priests as they used to be.

We also learn by an item in a certain publication that all crosses have now been removed from all military chapels in this country. It appears that things are moving fast to end the long reign of the priests.

Search Magazine for April, 1967, carried an interesting article titled "I'm a Teenaged Atheist," showing that the anthropomorphic God of Christianity is falling to impress the younger generation, and that religion has nothing of importance to offer any one but the clergy and those who promote it for profit.

Chapter No. 6
Ancient Religions

Perhaps no loss resulting from the destruction of ancient literature by the Christian Priesthood to hide their great fraud, had been more disastrous than that of the liturgic literature of Paganism. And that was the very literature the Christian Priesthood feared most and tried the hardest to destroy.

About all that escaped destruction were a few mystic formulas quoted incidentally by Pagan or Christian authors, and a few fragments of hymns in honor of the ancient gods.

To form some concept of what these lost rituals may have been, we must consider their imitation contained in the chorus of tragedies, and to the parodies comic authors sometimes produced. Or look up in the books of magic the plagiarisms that writers of incantations may have committed.

But all this gives us only a dim reflection of the religious ceremonies. Shut out of the sanctuary like profane outsiders, we hear only the indistinct echo of the sacred songs, and not even in our imagination can be attendant at the celebration of the mysteries.

We cannot penetrate into the intimacy of the religious life of the ancient pagans. And it's certain that if a fortunate windfall could give us possession of some sacred book of Paganism, its revelations would shock the Christian World. For they would disclose where Christianity got its gods.

Then we could witness the performance of those mystic dramas whose symbolic acts commemorated the passion of the gods. In company with the worshippers, we could sympathize with their sufferings, lament their death, and share in the joy of their return to life.

In those vast collections of archaic rites that hazily perpetuated the memory of abolished creeds, we would find traditional formulas couched in obsolete language that was scarcely understood: naïve prayers conceived by the faith of the early ages, sanctified by the devotion of past centuries, and almost ennobled by the joys and sufferings of past generations.

We could also read those ancient hyms in which philosophic thought found expression in sumptuous allegories, or humbled itself before the omnipotence of the infinite — poems of which only a few stoic effusions celebrating the creative or destructive fires, or expressing a complete surrender to divine fate, can give us some idea.

We would feel this great loss less keenly had we at least the works of Greek and Latin mythographers on the subject of the ancient divinities, like the voluminous works published in the second century by Eusebius and Pallas on the Mysteries of Mythra.

The treatises on mythology that have been preserved, deal almost entirely with the ancient Hellenic fables, made famous by classic writers, to the neglect of the Oriental religions.

All we find in literature on this subject are a few incidental remarks and passing allusions which the Mother Church did not deem necessary to destroy. Written history is incredibly scanty in that respect, due to the censorship of the Church.

It's exceedingly important to realize clearly that there is no period in the whole history of the Roman Empire concerning which the world is so little informed as that of the 3rd Century A.D.

Why is this so? Because that is the time when the clever work was done that gave birth to the Roman State Church. That surprising event occurred in the early part of the 4th Century, and resulted primarily from Constantine's efforts to improve the religious conditions of his empire.

There was then no Bible. The four Gospels of the New Testament had not yet been written, for up to that time Christ Jesus was unknown. The Gospels were not written until after he was invented. And that invention happened nearly three hundred years after the time when he was supposed to have lived, and performed his magic, and was crucified, died on the cross, and was resurrected, to become the Lord and Savior of Humanity.

What a shock it would be to those ancient worshippers of a nature god that symbolized certain powers and products of Creation, if they could come back and see how we modern people had modernized their mythology by personifying their symbolical god that represented the death of vegetation in the fall and its resurrection in the spring.

We have ignorantly transformed an ancient symbol into a virgin born god and had him crucified, put to death on a cross, buried, and resurrected to be worshipped by millions of deceived people as the Lord and savior of mankind.

That is the hidden story of what Constantine and the priests of his empire did in their fraudulent work during the early part of the 4th Century. And the knowledge of the perpetration of that greatest fraud in all history uncovers the secret why not a word of the story appeared in history until the 4th Century.

There was no need for the story until the Church was born. And after the birth of the Church it became necessary to conceal, to obliterate and to destroy all literature and all history covering the first three hundred years of the AD epoch, to hide from the eyes of the world what Constantine and the priests of his empire had done.

And to think that in the last fifty years scores of books have been written by Christian authors in their attempt to show that their Jesus was a real man, and not a mythical invention. No one needs to write books to show that Julius Caesar or George Washington were real men who actually lived. And yet they were almost nothing compared to what the gospel Jesus is pictured to be.

But the deceived world is gradually gaining light. The hidden data being uncovered by unorthodox writers increases the value of the information by epigraphical and archeological documents, whose number is constantly increasing, due to the good work of the researchers, which work is no longer prohibited by the Church because of its loss of the great power which it used to have, and which it exercised most ruthlessly.

The ancient inscriptions that have been uncovered by these research workers possess a certainty as to various events that are so frequently absent in the work of common writers.

The important work of archeology is rapidly filling the blanks left by the written tradition. The ancient monuments, especially the artistic ones, have not yet all been collected with sufficient care, nor interpreted with sufficient method.

The new knowledge gained enables us to draw reliable conclusions as to dates of propagation and disappearance of various ancient religions, their extent, their doctrines, and the social rank of their votaries, the sacred hierarchy and sacerdotal personal, the constitution of the religious communities, the offerings made to the gods, and the ceremonies performed in their honor. In short, important conclusions as to the secular and profane history of these religions, and, in a certain measure, their ritual.

True to the traditions of the Orient, the ancient knowledge edified and directed at the same time. It told in cycles of pictures the history of the gods and of the world, or it expressed in symbols the subtle conceptions of theology and even certain doctrines of ancient science, — for instance, that the Universe is basically constituted of four principal elements, designated as Fire, Air, Water and Earth, and symbolized in all countries of the ancient world by *The Mysterious Sphinx,* (available at www.frontlinebookpublishing.com) as expounded by us in our work of that title.

But to understand the hidden messages in the mystic book of the ancient world, whose pages are scattered thru our museums, we must search for the Key, which is concealed in the older religions of Egypt, Babylonia and Persia.

As we become able to translate more correctly the hieroglyphics of the Nile, the cuneiform tables of Mesopotamia, and the scared books of the Parseeism or Parsiism, we profit greatly in our researches in the acquirement of that knowledge which is so seriously needed.
In Syria, the discovery of the Aramaic and Phoenician inscriptions, and the excavations made in ancient temples, have supplied some of the deficiency of the data in the Bible and in the Greek writings on Semitic Paganism.

Even the uplands of Anatolia, in Asia Minor, are giving up to the explorers important buried secrets, altho most of the great sanctuaries are still buried underground.

We have not yet been able to weld together all the links of this long chain. The orientalist and the philologists cannot yet shake hands across the Mediterranean.

We raise one corner of the veil of Isis, and scarcely guess a part of the mysterious revelations that were reserved for a pious and chosen few. Yet we have already reached a sumit from which we can gaze over the broad field which our successors some day will clear, provided the present course is not interrupted by some new power that may eventually replace Christianity, and also be just as deceitful.

Chapter No. 7
Nature Worship

"God is a blank tablet, on which there is nothing save that which thou thyself hast written"*(Martin Luther, 1438-1546).*
"Whenever knowledge takes a step forward, God recedes a step backward" *(Alfred Naquet, 1834).*

"God made man, then man began making gods and has never stopped. ... The automatic agencies of the Universe that created the sun, moon and stars, also created gods and angels, ghosts and devils, monkeys and men" *(Doctor James Clark of London, in Eternal Time).*

And so the search for God goes on and on, with negative results that seem to discourage no one, and especially the priests, who could not deceive their dupes without their god.

To find the gods and goddesses of our ancient ancestores, we need only to look to the forms and forces of Creation. The sun, the moon, the planets, the stars, the sky, the sea, the earth, the night, the dawn, the clouds, the wind, the storm, the lightning and thunder, the seasons and vegetation etc.

It has become an established fact that these forms and forces of creation were personified and worshipped in the temples of the ancient world.

The words that denoted these forms and forces would logically signify living things and living persons. And from personification to deification the steps would be short, and the cunning priests would attend to that.

All the expressions that had been attached to living forms and natural forces would remain as the description of personal and anthropomorphic gods, and every word would become an attribute. And all thoughts, once grouped around any object, would branch off into distinct personifications.

Naturally, the glorious Sun was the lord of light, the driver of the chariot of the day, and the toiler for the sons of the earth. Then in the evening, after a hard struggle, he would sink down to rest.

Then the lord of light would be Phoibos Apollo, while Helios would remain enthroned in the fiery chariot, and his toils and struggles would be transferred to Hercules. The voilet clouds which greeted his rising and saw his setting, would now be represented by herds of cattle that feed in earthly pastures.

There would be various other expressions that would still remain as floating phrases, and attached to any of the deities. Tehse would gradually be converted by the priests into incidents in the life of the heroes, and woven at length into systematic narratives. Finally, these gods or heroes, and the incidents of their mythical career, would each receive a local habitation and a name. And the priests would see that these remained as real history after the origin and meaning of the words had either been wholly or partially forgotten.

For proof of these assertions, we have only to examine the Vedic poems, which furnish indisputable evidence that such as this was the origin and development of Babylonian and Egyptian mythology. In these poems, the names of most of the gods indicate natural objects which, if endued with life, have been transformed to human personality.

In the poems, Eos is still the goddess of the dawn. As morning twilight appears, she rises from the couch of her spouse, Tithonus, and ascends in a Chariot drawn by horses from the river Oceanus, which encircles the world, to herald the splendor of the new born sun.

The cattle of Helios are still light-coloured clouds, which the dawn leads out the pastures of the sky. There the idea of Hercules has not yet been separated from the image of the toiling sun, and the glory of the life-giving Helios has not been transferred to the god of Delos and Pytho.

In the Vedas the myths of Endymion, of Kephalos and Prokris, of Orpheus and Eurydike, are exhibited in the form of detached mythical phrases, which furnish for each their germ.

This analysis could be extended indefinitely; but the conclusion can be only that in the Vedic terminology appears the foundation not only of the legends of Hellas, but of the somber mythology of the Scandivanian and the Teuton. Both have grown up largely from names grouped around the sun. But the former has been grounded on those expressions which describe the recurrence of day and night, and the latter on the great tragedy of nature, in the alternation of summer and winter.

Of this vast mass of solar myths, some have emerged into independent legends, others have furnished the foundation of whole epics, and others have remained simply as floating tales whose intrinsic beauty no poet has wedded in his verse.

The evidence obtained from an examination of language in its several forms, leaves no room for any doubt that the general system of mythology has been traced to its fountain-head.

In spite of the clever work of the priesthood, we can no longer close our eyes to the fact, that there was a stage in the history of speech, during which all the abstract words, in common use today, were utterly unknown; when men had formed no notion of virtue or prudence, of thought and intellect, of slavery and freedom, but spoke only of the man who was strong, who could point out the way to others, and choose one thing out of many; of the man who was not bound to any one, and was able to do as he pleased.

That even this stage was not the earliest in the history of language is the growing opinion amoug philologists. But for the comparison of legends, current in different countries, it's unnecessary to carry the search any further back.

Speech without words denoting abstract qualities implies a condition of thought in which men were only awakening to a sense of the objects which surrounded them, and points to a time when the world was to them full of strange sights and sounds, some beautiful, some bewildering, some terrific, when, in short, they knew little about themselves beyoud the vague consciousness of their existence, and little of the phenomena of the external world.

In such a state, men could but attribute to all that they saw, or touched, or heard, a life which was like their own in its consciousness, its pleasure, and its sufferings; and they were right. That power of sympathizing with nature, which we are apt to regard as a special gift of the poet, was then shared by all.

This sympathy was not the result of any effort. It was natural and inseparably connected with the words which rose to their lips. It implied no special purity of heart or mind; it pointed to no mythical paradise, where shepherds knew not how to wrong or oppress or torment one another.

We say the light of the rising sun rests on the mountains; they said the sun was greeting his bride, as naturally as our own poet would speak of the sunlight as clasping the earth, or the moonbeams as kissing the face of the sea.

We have then a stage of speech corresponding to a stage in the history of the human mind in which all sensible objects were regarded as being endued with conscious life. The varying phases of that life were described as factually as they described their own feeling of pleasure or suffering; and hence every phrase became a picture.

So long as the condition of their life remained unchanged, they knew what that picture meant, and ran no risk of confusing one with another. Then they had but to describe the things they saw, felt, or heard in order to keep an inexhaustible store of phrases descibing the facts of the world from their point of view.

This language was the natural result of observation not less keen than that by which the inductive philosopher extorts the secrets of the natural world; nor was its range much narrower.

Each object received its own measure of attention, and no one phenomenon was so treated as to leave no room for others in their turn. They could not fail to observe the changes of days and years, of growth and decay, of winter and summer, of calm and storm. But the objects which so changed were to them living things. And the rising and setting of the sun, the return of winter and summer, the growth and decay of vegetation, became a drama of creative action, in which the actors were either their enemies or their friends.

That this is a logical review of the facts in the history of the human mind, philology alone would prove. But not a few of these phrases have come down to us in their earliest form, and point to a long-buried stratum of language of which they are the fragments.

These relics exhibit in their germs the myths that later became the legends of gods and heroes with human forms, and furnished the foundation of the epic poems of the world.

The mythical language of anicient man had no partialities. And if the career of the Sun occupies a large extent of the horizon, we cannot fairly simulate ignorance of the cause.

Men so placed would not fail to put into words the thoughts and emotions aroused in them by the varying phases of that mighty globe on which we, no less than they, feel that our very life depends. And proof of this is easily found in the fact that the face of the earth would become like a barren rock if the sun should set and never rise again.

Thus developed a multitude of expressions which described the sun as the ghost of the night, as the destroyer of the darkness, as the lover of the dawn — of phrases which would go on and speak of the Sun as killing the dew with his spears, and of forsaking the dawn as he rose in the heavens.

The fact that the fruits and flowers of the earth were called forth by the warmth of the Sun, could fined expression in words which spoke of him as the friend and benefactor of man; while the constant recurrence of his work would lead men to describe him as being constrained to toil for others, as deemed to travel over many lands, and as finding everywhere things on which he could bestow his love, or which he might destroy with his power.

Again, his journey might be across cloudless skies, or amid alternations of calm and storm. His light might break fitfully thru the dark clouds, or be hidden for many weary hours, or burst forth at last with glowing splendor as he sank down in the western sky. He would then be described as facing many dangers and enemies, but none of whom were able to arrest his course.

Then as the veil was rent at eventide, they would speak of the chief, who had long remained still, girding on his armor;

or of a wanderer throwing off his disguise, and seizing his bow or spear to smite his foes; of the invincible warrior whose face shone with the flush of victory when the fight is finished, as he greets the fair-haired Dawn who closes the day as she began it.

To the wealth of the images thus lavished upon the daily life and death of the sun, there would be hardly any limit. He was the child of the morning, the warrior of the day, and the victor of the night.

And so with the varoius sights and sounds in nature. The darkness of night produced a feeling of vague horror and dread, and the return of day light cheered them with a sense of gladness. And thus the Sun who scattered the black shades of night would be the mighty champion doing battle with the beast that lurked in its dark hiding-place.

As the sun performed his journey day by day thru the tractless heavens, the state of the seasons is changed. The buds and blooms of spring time appear and expand into flowers and fruits of summer, and on the approach of winter the leaves wither and fall.

Thus the daughter of the earth would be regarded as dying or as dead, as severed from her mother during the weary winter months, not to be restored to her again until the time for her to return from the dark land when spring time would once more arrive.

As no other power but that of the Sun can resurrect dead vegetation to life, this child of the earth would be represented as buried in sleep from which the touch of the Sun alone could arouse her, when he slays the frost and cold which lie as snakes around her motionless form.

These phases of nature would furnish the germs of myths or legends teeming with human feeling. As soon as the meaning of the phrases were wholly or partially forgotten, it was inevitable that on the infancy of the race, man should attribute to all sensible objects the same kind of life which he himself was conscious of possessing. And our vaunted science has produced no evidence yet to show that they were wrong in the matter of life.

When we turn to the Bible we find the Book of Psalms, which is nothing more than a song-book of praise of the various phases of Creation, much of which is devoted to the Sun. But the priests invented a terminology in their effort to lead the uninformed mind away from the Sun and to their mythical God. We quote:

"O clap your hands, all ye people; shout unto God with the voice of triumph. For the Lord (Sun) most high is terrible; he is a great King over all the earth" *(Psalms 47:1, 2)*.

"It is a good thing to give thanks unto the lord, and to sing praises unto thy name, O most High. To show forth thy loving-kindness in the morning, and thy faithfulness every night" *(Psalms 92:1, 2)*.

"The Lord reigneth; let the earth rejoice; let the multitude of isles be glad thereof. Clouds and darkness are round about him, righteousness and judgement are the habitation of his throne. A fire goeth before him, and burneth up his enemies round about. His lightnings enlightened the world; the earth saw, and trembled. The hills melted like wax at the presence of the Lord of the whole earth. The heavens declare his righteousness, and all the people see his glory" *(Psalms 97:1-6)*.

The priests make their living by pulling these Sun Gods and Nature Gods down to the earth and selling them to the gullible masses, who wordhip them as Divine Beings.

Chapter No. 8
Cybele And Attis

History informs us that the first Oriental religion adopted by the Romans was that of Cybele and Attis, goddess and god of Phrygia.

The people of Pessinus and Mount Ida worshipped Cybele, who was called the Magna Mater Deum Ida, and the history of this worship in Italy covers six hundred years. And its enlightening to find that, as we trace each phase of the transformation invented by the priesthood, how the religion in the course of time was cleverly changed from a collection of primitive nature beliefs into a system of Spiritualized Mysteries designed to confuse the minds of the people.

But the success of this religion in the Latin world was due to a chance condition. In 205 B. C. Hannibal, vanquished but still threatening, made his last stand in the mountains of Bruttium, and for some mysterious reason repeated torrents of stones scared the Romans.

When the oracles were consulted in regard to this prodigy, they asserted that the enemy would be driven from Italy if the Great Mother Cybele were brought to Rome.

Only the Sybils had the power to avert the evils prophesied by them. Help had to come to Italy from Asia Minor, and in this critical situation their scared poem recommended as a remedy the adoption of their suggestion.

In token of his friendship, King Attalus presented the ambassadors of the Roman Senate with the Black Aerolite (Holy Stone), supposed to be the adobe of the goddess, which this ruler had shortly before transferred from Pessinus to Pargamum.

According to the mandate from the Oracle, the Holy Stone was received at Ostia by the best people of the land, an honor accorded to Scipio Nasica — and carried by the most esteemed matrons to Palatine, where, hailed with the cheers of the multitude and surrounded by the fumes of incense, it was solemnly installed.

This triumphal entry was later glorified by marvellous legends, and the poets joined in by edifying miracles that had occurred during Cybele's voyage.

In the same year Scipio transferred the seat of war to Africa, and Hannibal, forced to meet him there, was defeated at Zama (now Tunisia).

So the predictions of the Sybils had come true, and Rome was free from the long Punic menace.

Cybele was accordindly honored in recognition of the help she had rendered. A fine temple was erected to her on the sumit of the Palatine, and every year a celebration, enhanced by scenic plays, commemorated the date of dedication of the sanctuary and the arrival of the goddess.

This Asiatic religion that had been received in Rome, could even then look back to a long period of development. It combined belief of various origins, and contained primitive usage of the religion of Anatolia, some phases of which have servived unto this day in spite of Christianity's efforts to obliterate them.

Like the Kizil-bash peasants of today, the ancient people of the peninsula met on the summits of mountains covered with woods which no ax had desecrated, and celebrated their festal days.

They believed that Cybele, the Great Mother of the Gods, lived on the tops of Ida and Berecyntus, and the perennial pines, in conjunction with the early maturing almond trees, were the sacred trees of Attis, the ancient fertility god beloved by Cybele.

Besides trees, the people worshipped stones or meteors that had fallen from Pessinus to Paragmum and thence to Rome.

The Phrygians at an early period came from Thrace and inserted themselves like a wedge into the old Anatolian races, and cleverly adopted the gods of their new country by identifying them with their own, after the common practice of pagan nations.

Thus, Attis became one with the Dionysus-Sabazius of the conquerers, or at least assumed some of his characteristics.

The Thracian Dionysus was a god of vegetation. Wooded summits, dense forests, ivy-clad caverns were his haunts. Mortals who wanted to know the divinity ruling these solitudes, had to observe the life of his kingdom, and to guess the god's nature from the phenomena thru which he manifested his powers.

Observing the creeks descend in noisy cascades, or hearing the braying of cattle in the highlands, or the strange sounds of the gale thru the forest, the Thracians thought they heard the calls of the god of that empire, and imagined he was fond of extravagant leaps and of wild roaming over the wooded hills.

This conception of Nature inspired their religion. For the best way that mortals can ingratiate themselves with a divinity was to imitate him, and, as far as possible, to make their lives resemble his.

How well that same sentiment appears in the case of the god Jesus, who said, "If any man will come after me, let him deny himself, and take up his cross, and follow me" *(Matthew 16:24).*

And so the Thracians endeavored to attain the divine religion that transported their Dionysus, and hoped to realize their purpose by following their invisible yet ever-present god in his chase over mountains and thru forests.

We of today regard this belief as stupid and ludicrous; but what are we doing that is any higher and wiser in the religious field?

In the Phrygian religion appeared the same beliefs and rites, hardly modified at all, with this one exception: That Attis, the god of vegetation, was united with the goddess of the earth instead of living in sullen loneliness.

When the wild tempest was thrashing the timber of the Berecyntus or Ida, it was Cybele travelling in her chariot, drawn by roaring lions, mourning the death of Attis.

A crowd of worshippers followed her thru the woods, mingling their cries with the shrill sound of flutes, with the dull beat of tambourines, the rattling of castanets and the dissonance of brass cymbals.

Intoxicated with the shouting and the roaring of the instruments, excited by their inpetuous advance, and breathless and panting, they surrendered to the raptures of a sacred enthusiasm.

Eighty years ago we withnessed somewhat similar scenes, in this modern civilization, at the religious of negroes in the city where we lived. We still live in ancient days so far as religion is concerned. But the deceived masses don't know it.

Climate also has a certain effect on the people. The climate of the Anatolian uplands was one of extremes. Its winters were long and cold, and the spring showers developed a sudden growth of vegetation that was soon scorched by the hot summer sun.

The abrupt contrast of nature, generous and sterile, radiant and bleak in turn, causes excesses of happiness and sadness that were unknown in more favourable regions, where the ground is never buried under snow, nor scorched by the heat of the sun.

The Phrygians mourned the long death of the vegetation, and when the fresh verdure reappeared in March, they surrendered to the excitement of tumultuous rejoicing.

In Asia Minor certain rites that had been unknown in Thrace or else observed in milder form, expressed the vehemence of those opposing feelings. In the midst of their violent orgies, and after wild dances, some of the more excited worshippers wounded themselves, and, becoming stanchless with the sight of their own blood, with which they besprinkled their altars, they belived they were uniting themselves with their god, or else, arriving at a paroxysm of frenzy, they sacrificed their virility to the gods, as some Russian dissenters still do now.

These emasculated men became the priests of Cybele, and were called Galli, being men who castrated themselves in identification with the Goddess.

And now we condense the following from a Dictionary of classical antiquities, first published in 1891:

Cybele, Great Mother of the Gods, a goddess representing the (1) powers of Nature, and the (2) Art of agriculture, was worshipped upon mountains in Mysia, Lydia, and Phrygia.

In the former character, she represented the procreative powers of Nature; and in the latter, she symbolized the cultivation of the fields, together with other forms of social progress and civilization, which depended upon these. Thus she was regarded as the founder of towns and cities, and so art represented her as crowned with a diadem of towers.

The original home of this religion was the Phrygian Pessinus, on the river Sangarius, in the district later known as Galatia, where the goddess was called Agdistis, from a Holy Stone named Agdus, upon Mount Dindymus above the town.

On this mountain from which the goddess derived the name of Dindymene, stood her earliest sanctuary, as well as her oldest effigy (a stone that had fallen heaven), and the grave of her beloved Attis. Her priests, the emasculated Galli, here enjoyed almost royal honor. Her mythical train was formed by the Corybantes. These were said to accompany her over the wooden hills, with lighted torches and wild dances, amid the resounding music of flutes, horns, drums and cymbals.

After these the priests of Cybele were called Corybantes, and the festivals of the goddess were celebrated in similar origies, in the frenzy of which the participators wounder one another, or, like Attis, mutilated themselves.

From Asia Minor this religion drifted into Greece, and for political reasons, it was introduced into Rome in 204 B.C., at the command of a Sibylline oracle, for the purpose of driving Hannibal out of Italy.

An embassy was sent to bring the Holy Stone from Pessinus. A festival was founded in honor of the goddess, to be held on April 4-9; and in the year 217 a temple on the Palatine was dedicated to her. The service was performed by a Phrygian priest, a Phrygian priestess, and a number of Galli (emasculated priests of Cybele), who were allowed to pass in procession thru the city in accordance with their native rules.

The worship of Cybele gained many followers, and under the early Empire a fresh festival was instituted, from March 15-27, with the observance of mourning, followed by the most extravagant rejoicing.

In the first half of the 2nd Century, A.D., the Taurobolia and Criobolia were added. In these ceremonies the people concerned went thru the form of baptism with the blood of bulls and rams, killed in sacrifice, with the object of cleansing them from pollution and bringing about a new birth.

All these demonstrations of an extreme worship should not cause us to slight the power of the feeling that inspired them. The sacred ecstasy, the voluntary mutilation of the body, and the eagerly sought suffering, mainfested an ardent longing for deliverance from subjection to carnal lust, and a fervent desire to free the Soul from the bonds of matter.

The ascetic tendencies went so far as to create a kind of begging monachism   the metragyrtes. They also harmonized with some of the concepts of renunciation taught by Greek philosophy. And at an early period Hellenic theologians took an interest in this devotion that attracted and repelled at the same time.

Timotheus the Emuolpid, who was one of the founders of the Alexandrian religion of Serapis, derived from the ancient Phrygian myths the inspiration for his essays on religious reform.

The votaries of Cybele began at a very remote period to practice "mysteries," in which the initiates were made acquainted, by degrees, with a wisdom that was always considered divine, but underwent peculiar variations in the course of time.

Cybele was supposed to traverse the mountains riding on a lion, or in a chariot drawn by lions. In art, she was usually represented enthroned between lions, with the mural crown on her head and a small drum in her hand.

We here condense from a Dictionary of Classical Antiquities the story of Attis: — A mythical personage in the worship of the Phrygian goddess Cybele. The son of this goddess, according to the story, had been mutilated by the almond-tree. After eating its fruit, Nana, daughter of the river Sangarius, bought forth a boy, whom she exposed. He was brought up first amoung the wild goats of the forest, and afterwards by some shepherds, and grew up so handsome that Agdistis fell in love with him. Wishing to wed the daughter of the king of Pessinus in Phrygia, he was driven to madness by the goddess. He then fled to the mountains, and destroyed his manhood at the foot of a pine-tree, which received his spirit, while from his blood sprang violets to garland the tree.

Agdistis besought Zeus that the body of her beloved one might know no corruption. Her prayers were heard; a tomb to Attis was raised on Mount Dindymus in the sanctuary of Cybele, the priests of which had to suffer emasculation for the sake of Attis.

Chapter No. 9
Ancient Worship

We have observed that the Roman accepted and adopted theological and cosmological doctrines of an ancient brand of crude and primitive religious concepts, such as the worship of stones, trees, and beasts. That knowledge discloses some intimation of the manner in which gods and religious systems were born.

Besides this superstitious fetichism, it involved ceremonies that were both sensual and ribald, including all the wild and mystic rites of the bacchanalia which the public authorities of Rome did not approve.

When the Roman Senate learned more about the divinity imposed upon it by the Sibyls, it must have been somewhat embarrassed. For the enthusiastic transport of the somber fanaticism of Phrygian worship contrasted violently with the calm dignity and respectable reserve of the offical religion, and excited the minds off the people to a dangerous degree.

The emasculated Galli were objects of contempt and disgust, and what in their own opinion was a meritorious act, was made a crime punishable by law, at least under the empire.

The authorities hesitated between the respect due to the powerful goddess that had delivered Rome from the Carthaginians and the reverence for the *mos mariorum*. They resolved the difficulty by completely isolating the new religion. All citizens were forbidden to join with the priesthood of the foreign goddess, or to participate in her origies. The rites according to which the great Mother Cybele was to be worshipped were by Phrygian priests and priestesses.

Kept closely under control, the Phrygian worship led an obscure existence until the establishment of the empire. That closed the first period of its history at Rome. It attracted attention only on certain holidays, when its priests marched in the streets in procession, dressed in motley costumes, loaded with jewelry, and beating tambourines.

On those days the Senate granted them the right to go from house to house to collect funds for their temples. The remainder of the year they confined themselves to the sacred enclosure of the Palatine, celebrating foreign ceremonies in a foreign language.

They created so little notice during this period, that almost nothing is known of their practice or creed. But the Phrygian religion stayed alive in spite of police surveillance. A breach had been made in the cracked wall of the old Roman principles, thru which the entire Orient finally gained ingress.

After the establishment of the empire, the apprehensive distrust in which the worship of Cybele and Attis had been held, gave way to marked favor and the original restrictions were abolished. Then Roman citizens were chosen for archigalli, and the holidays of the Phrygian deities were solemnly and officially celebrated in Italy with even more pomp than had been displyed at Pessinus.

Emperor Claudius was the author of this change. He introduced a cycle of holidays that were celebrated from March 15th to the 27th, the beginning of spring and the time of the revival of vegetation, personified by Attis.

The various acts of this grand religious drama are well known. The prelude was a procession of cannophori, or reed-bearers, on the 15th. They commemorated Cybele's finding of Attis, who, according to the legends, had been exposed as a child on the banks of the Sangarius, the largest river in Phrygia. This ceremony may have been the transformation of the ancient phallephory intended to guarantee the fertility of the fields.

The ceremonies proper began with the equinox. A pine tree was felled and carried to the temple of the palatine by a brotherhood called the "treebearers." Wrapped like a corpse in woolen bands and garlands of violets, this treee represented Attis as being dead.

This god was originally only the spirit of the plants, and the honors given to the "March-tree" in front of the imperial palace perpetuated a very ancient agrarian rite of the Phrygian peasants.

The next day was a day of sadness and abstinence, and the followers fasted and mourned the defunct god.

The 24th bore the significant name of Sanguis in the calendars. It was the celebration of the funeral of Attis, whose manes were appeased by means of libations of blood, as was done for any mortal.

Mingling their piercing cries with the shrill sound of flutes, the Galli flagellated themselves and cut themselves and the neophytes performed the supreme sacrifice of emasculation with the aid of a sharp stone, being insensible to pain in their frenzy.

Then followed a mysterious vigil during which the mystic was supposed to be united as a new Attis with the great goddess.

On March 25th there was a sudden transition from the shouts of despair to delirious jubilation, the Hilaria.

When springtime arrived, Attis awoke from his winter-sleep of death, and the rejoicing created by his resurrection exploded in boisterous celebration, wanton masqueredes, and luxurious banquets.

This is where the Christian Fathers found some of the story of the Resurrection and they applied the process to their own Jesus, but in a far different manner.

After twenty-four hours of an indispensable rest (requietio), the festivities ended, on the 27th, with a long and gorgeous procession thru the streets of Rome and surrouding country districts. Under a constant rain of flowers, the silver statue of Cybele was taken to the river Almo and bathed and purified according to the ancient rite (lavatio).

The worship of the Mother of the Gods had penetrated into the Hellenic nations long before it was received at Rome. But in Greece it assumed a peculiar form and lost most of its barbarous character.

The Greek mind felt an aversion to the dubious nature of Attis, the Manga Mater, who is different from her Hellenized sister, penetrated into all Latin provines and imposed herself upon them with the Roman religion.

As late as the 4th Century, during the very time when the Roman State Church was being established by Constantine, the chariot of Cybele, drawn by steers, was led in great state thru the fields and vineyards of Autun in order to stimulate their fertility.

Ancient authors have described the impression made on the masses by these magnificent processions, in which Cybele passes along in her chariot, preceded by musicians playing captivating melodies, by priests wearing gorgeous constumes covered with amulets, and by the long line of votaries and members of the fraternities, all barefoot and wearing their insignia.

All of this created only a fleeting impression upon the neophyte, but as soon as he entered the temple, he was affected by a deeper sensation. He heard the pathetic story of the goddess seeking the body of her lover, cut down in the prime of life, like the grass of the field, he saw the bloody funeral services in which the cruel death of the young god was mourned, and heard the joyful hymns of triumph, and the gay songs that greeted his resurrection to life.

By a skilfully arranged gradation of feelings, the spectators were thrilled with a state of rapturous ecstasy. Feminine devotion in particular found enjoyment in these ceremonies, and the Great Mother, the fecund and generous goddess, was especially worshipped by women.

Peolple founded great hopes on the pious practice of this religious system. They were led to believe in the immortality of the soul. Just as Attis died and returned to life again every year, these devotees believed they would be born into a new life after death. In fact, that was the essence of the entire system.

One of the sacred hymns said: "Take courage, oh ye mystics, for the god is saved; and for you also will come salvation from your trails."

Even the funeral ceremonies were affected by the strenght of this belief. Graves have been found adorned with earthenware statuettes representing the god Attis. And even in Germany the grave-stones are frequently decorated with the figure of a young man in oriental costume, leaning upon a stick (pedum), who represented Attis.

We are ignorant of the conception of immortality held by the oriental disciples of the god Attis. Like the votaries of

Sabazius, may be they belived that they were permitted to participate with Hermes Psychopompos in a geat celestial feast, for which they were prepared by the sacred repasts of the mysteries.

We have reviewed one of the many systems of ancient religion that preceded Christianity, and furnished the pattern from which Christianity was copied, the god Jesus was just as mythical as the god Attis, who furnished the picture used by the christian Fathers to invent their Jesus. All the gods of religion fall into the same category, and are invented and employed by the priests to deceive and control the gullible masses. If our Christian Fathers look upon those ancient people as being superstitious heathens what are we? The Christian system is just as unsound and fallacious as any of the ancient world.

Chapter No. 10
Rome

In the first Century A.D. the Roman Empire dominated the known world. The government was tolerant. The people were permitted to observe their different customs and religions, and the individual states had their own local self-governments.

It was then the happiest world known in history. "To be a Roman was greater than to be a king," was a common saying. The people were ignorant, but free. They were permitted their home pleasures and prejudices. Seasons of plenty they considered to be the work of good spirits — and bad years were the work of evil spirits, the people thought.

They were taught nothing about the operation of the immutable laws of Creation. They were slaves of the priests. Ignorance breeds fear and superstition, and these are the foundation of all religion. The priests have always been careful to see that the intelligence of the multitude does not rise above that low level.

The Roman Emperors encouraged everything that pacified the people and protected the interest of the empire. They were indifferent to the various forms of religious worship, some of which veered toward the worship of the rules and the state. Temples were built to Augustus and Rome.

But after the Roman State Church was established in the 4th Century, a marked change cleverly appeared. The world does not know that the entire Christian services ritual was adopted from the different pagan religions so that the people would not notice any change.

The gospel Jesus taught no ritual, nor had he a ceremonial. The ignorant people could not understand the niceties of creeds, dogmas, and rituals, but they could see the gaudy and inspiring performances of the priests and their retinues. These were designed to impress the masses; and so they embraced the gods that attracted them.

Realizing the success of this scheme, the Church resorted to gorgeous decorations, robes of bright colours, cymbals and show, unusual festivals and pageantry, hymns and altars, lighted candles, and religious mysteries were introduced. These changed the ignorant masses from the worship of pagan gods to the worship of a Jesus. It made no difference to them. A god was a god.

And in this way the Church rapidly gained power at Rome, and it early began mildly to assert its authority. Its first recorded act was when Victor, Bishop of Rome, commanded the church of Asia Minor to celebrate Easter on the same day that Rome did. They responded by telling Victor to mind his own business. He was furious, and threatened to excommunicate the bishops. And they just laughed.

For thirty years after that Rome gave no more orders. Pope Callistus, a shrewd ex-slave of vile character, then declared himself "the supereme Pontiff." That created not a ripple.

Rome's persistent and increased domineering conduct made the outside churches only more hostile. They drifted further apart and split into many sects. There was yet no real head, no controlling body, but few churches, no Bible, no uniform creed. Each priest delivered his own doctrine. More than eighty conflicting beliefs existed. A thousand conflicting documents were read at meetings, or taken as texts by the priests.

The future of the Church at this time looked gloomy. Something had to be done, and it was done.

Constantine, the Roman Emperor, had carefully watched everything with increasing alarm. The bitter conflict between the different faiths worried him. He saw them splitting his empire into warring, factions. He realized that if they were not checked, this course would destroy his empire, and he decided to end the conflict. He would have one church and banish the others.

He acted quickly, and, to the church, unexpectedly. And the council of bishops he assembled, acting under his orders, decreed the Christ Jesus sect to be the official state religion.

This naturally started a religious revolution. Constantine met the situation by giving the new sect large sums of the tax money paid by the people, and building expensive temples for the Christ Jesus sect in most centers of his realm.

A great change swept over the empire. Droves of parasitical priests attached themselves to the Christ Jesus sect. The politicians, desiring regal favors, flocked to Christ Jesus. The weak and cowardly, thru fear, climbed on the band wagon. The pagan temples were closed, destroyed, or turned into Christian churches. Decrees of death faced the non-believers.

When the strange story of Christ Jesus was first introduced among the Romans, they mocked at the "Lord and Savior born in a manger." That attitude changed as they discovered how dangerous it was when Constantine promulgated the New Faith in official decrees, which the police and soldiers rigidly enforced.

Little did these Romans then dream that they and their children, for a thousand years, would see rivers reddened with their blood because of the Jesus whom they had mocked, and that their proud empire would sink in darkness as the Haughty Roman Empire rose to power, and, with Bible in one hand and bloody sword in the other, gradually clamp its galling yoke on the countries controlled by Rome.

And little did the Apostle Paul and his group realize that "the (ancient) gospel which was preached of me is not after man" *(Galatians 1:11, 12)*, would be revised and revamped to make a man of an ancient symbol, which represented the Spirit (Spark of Life) in all men *(Colossians 3: 11)*, and to make the Spiritual Resurrection to which he referred as a mystery *(1 Corinthians 15: 42, 51)*, the literal resurrection of a human corpse.

What a shock it had been to Paul had he been told that the Kingdom of God, which he declared could not be inherited by "flesh and blood" *(1 Corinthians 15:50)*, and which the Luke gospel said was within the body *(Luke 17: 21)*, would later receive into its folds the "flesh and blood" of the church.

Jesus, who is made to say — "Behold my hands and my feet, that it is I myself; handle me, and see; for a spirit hath not flesh and bones, as ye see me have" *(Luke 24: 39)*. What a Lie.

The ancient religion that had prevailed in all parts of the ancient world for thousands of years, was now suppressed. Ancient Philosophy and ancient history had to be destroyed to conceal the facts. Ancient temples had to be demolished, and the Masters of the ancient religion had to be converted or murdered .

This was a big job, but the work was done, and done well. Many of the Masters escaped by fleeing to the mountains, and there continued their work in secret.

The task of burning ancient literature, suppressing learning, and murdering dissenters continued until the latter part of the 6th Century, when the Dark ages, which lasted for a thousand years, began to settel over Europe, Asia Minor and Egypt.

Bolingbroke said, *"The scene of the Roman State Church has always been one of dissention, of hatred, of persecution, and of blood."*

Erasmus wrote: *"The Church was born in blood, grew in blood, succeeded in blood, and will disappear in blood."*

Tredwell declared that the Roman State Church forced its way to success by the suppression of philosophy and learning, by the point of the sword, and by mass murder.

This is a brief history of how the "Church Militant" was born, and how it succeeded in developing into a world power, reaching its peak of success during the darkest days of its reign.

And then something happened that changed everything so far as Christianity was concerned. In 1492, during the Dark Ages, came the Historic journey of Columbus, which showed that the earth is round, not flat as claimed by the Church.

That knowledge electrified the world. It flew so fast that the Church could not suppress it. It created the very condition the Church had foreseen and feared, and it had done all in its power to prevent Columbus from making that journey.

That event was the actual beginning of the Reformation, the Renaissance. It was bitterly fought by Romanism; but the battle was lost, and knowledge began to scatter the darkness in which the Church had felt secure.

Chapter No. 11
First Christians

"Then departed Barnabas to Tarsus, for the seek Saul. And when he had found him, he bought him to Antioch. And it came to pass that a whole year they assembled themselves with the church, and taught much people. And the disciples were called Christians first at Antioch" *(Acts 11:25, 26)*.

Who first called them Christians at Antioch? Why were they called Christians? Who put that statement in the Bible? Why was no evidence included to support the statement?

Many statements in the Bible are now know to be false. The makers of the Bible had a great scheme in mind when they made that book, and they made it to support that scheme and for no other purpose.

This Barnabus was not a disciple nor an apostle. He had never heard of the gospel Jesus. He was also known as Demas, and by that name is mentioned in the Bible several times *(Colossians 4:14, etc.)*. We have discovered who he was.

He went to get Saul, also known as Paul, and took him to Antioch because he was losing an argument about something with a certain magician known as Bar-Jesus, "a false prophet," and needed Paul's help.

And Paul moved in, took over, and came so decisively to the front, that henceforth, for the author of the Acts, he took the lead, and "Barnabas appears as his colleague" *(Acts 13:6-12)*.

Paul moved right out in the front and became the leader of the group that assembled themselves for a whole year at Antioch, and taught a certain doctrine to "much people." As a result of this teaching, the exact nature of which is not disclosed in the Bible, "the disciples were called Christians first at Antioch."

They were not disciples, nor apostles, and they had never heard of the gospel Jesus. Their leader was Paul, and that biblical data reveals a clue which we shall trace down, and present to the reader some surprising information. It will show that it was this Paul, and not the gospel Jesus, who was the man and the leader who really established the system that became known as Christianity.

But he knew it not, for the reason that the establishment of Christianity did not take place until after he had been dead nearly three hundred years.

Paul would have turned over in his grave had he known that as a result of his work as a preacher at Antioch and Ephesus, the Mother Church reached back nearly three hundred years, found his writings and found a record of him, and he became the gospel Jesus and his writings became the foundation of the New Testament.

Antioch was far from Jerusalem, situated on the left back of the Orontes, in Asia Minor, about 20 Miles from the Mediterranean Sea, and was founded as a Greek city in 300 B.C. by Seleuces Nicator.

Being so far from Jerusalem, how did it happen to become the "cradle of gentile Christianity?" Because of the Essenes, and Paul was their leader.

According to history, the Essenes were the first Christians. They suffered persecution by the Romans, and were thrown into the arena to be devoured by hungry lions.

This horrible persecution continued until the Council of Nicea, in 325 A.D. Then the Roman State Church was founded by Constantine, but still after that, the Essenes, then known as Manicheans, were still put to death by Roman churchmen, who stole their religion, and then transformed it to please their leader, the arch-murderer, Constantine.

Eusebius, bishop of Ceasarea, one of the leaders of the Church Fathers and who took a leading part in the establishment of Christianity, wrote the first history of Christianity in which he incorporated many falsehoods, and he admitted that the Essenes were the first Christians.

The real name of Saul of Tarsus, also called Paul in the Bible, was Apollonius, but his friends called Pol. He was the renown Pythagorean philosopher of the 1st Century A.D., the leader of the Essenes, also known as Nazarites or Nazarenes, and the hidden founder of the religious system that came to be called Christianity, as explained in our work titled *"Mystery   Man   of   the   Bible."*   (available   at www.frontlinebookpublishing.com)

Apollonius made two special journeys to India for the purpose of studying the Hindu religion. On his last return he introduced in the order of Essenes the Buddhist doctrines which he learned at the feet of his teacher, Iarchus. And the Hindu writings which he brought back with him were the origin of the Christian Gospels, with the vegetarian aspects eliminated, since these were obnoxious to the flesh-eating Roman   churchmen   and   their   degenerate   emperor, Constantine.

Pliny indicated the Essenes had a perennial colony on the shore of the Dead Sea, and estimated their number at 4000. They first appeared at the time of Jonathan the Maccabee, 161-144 B.C. But many authorities mention them as having existed in the days of Pythagoras, 500 B.C. Some writers give them a "dateless antiquity," which likewise traces their origin to the Hermetic Brotherhood of Egypt, and goes back to Atlantis. .

They gained their recruits in membership in two ways: Converts from the world at large, and adoption of orphan boys. Marriage was prohibited and denounced; they never married. So there was no accession in membership from their own children.

They had no special city of their own, and did not believe in urban life. They had agricultural communities, and agriculture was their regular pursuit. Except when toiling in the fields, they dressed in white garments, and especially when they assembled for their common meal.

In the morning, before sunrise, no one spoke a profane word. At sunrise they offered to the sun traditional forms of prayer. Then they went to work till the fifth hour, when the assembled and girded on a white linen garment, bathing in cold water. They entered the dining hall solemnly as if it were a temple, and sat down in the most profound silence. Each one received some bread and a dish with one mess. It was all stricity vegetarianism. Before and after a meal, a priest pronounced a prayer. Before returning to work, they discarded the garments which they had donned for the meal, and which they regarded as sacred, at evening they united for a second repast.

They believed in equality among men, in giving to those who were in want, and they avoided splendid garments and general cleaving to existing things. They rejected pleasure as an evil, and esteemed as a virtue the conquest over the passions. They were students of morality, and held that the soul, having descended from Aether, the most pure, and being drawn to the body by a certain natural attraction, remained in it as its prison.

They were in error in that case. The soul is the Vital Spark that builds and animates the body, and uses the body as an instrument to do the work that the body does in the visible world.

They kept no relation with the world beyond their community, and sought to serve society by giving it the example of a laborious life, a sincere piety, and a constant virtue which controlled all human passions. Those who entered the order had to bring to it all that they possessed; the property of the order, confided to administrators, was held in common and belonged to all; and there were no rich and no poor.

That mode of living seems to come close to what is termed Communism today, and if observed literally and completey, makes a group of people resemble a herd of cattle. Mead, in his *"Fragments of A Faith Forgotten,"* said: "For centuries before the Christian era, Essenic communities had dwelt on the shores of the Dead Sea for many centuries. Finding it impossible to carry out in ordinary life the strict regulations of the laws of purity, they had adopted the life of ascetic communism. Their strict observance of the purifactory discipline enacted by their order, compelled them to become a self- supporting community. They all work at a trade; they cultivated their own fields, made all the articles of dress they wore, and thus in every way avoided contact with those who did not observe the same rules."

And now we must consider further the rare man that lived and labored and performed the magic work attributed to the gospel Jesus. It took long searching to find him, but we found him and discovered that he was an outstanding philosopher who was the real leader of the group mentioned in the Bible, that assembled themselves for a whole year and taught "much people" at Antioch *(Acts. 11:25, 26)*.

The real name of this great man called Paul in the Bible, was Apollonius, of Tyana. He was born February 16, in the year 2 A.D. of wealthy parents, and died at the age of 98. He was highly educated in philosophy and the law of the prophets, and studied for six years under Euxenes (Eumenes) of Heracleis, learning the Pythagorean philoosphy of Creation.

Because of his incomparable record, the Roman State Church, after it was founded by Constantine in 325 A.D. selected him, after much consideration, to play the role of its Jesus.

Then came the necessary of hiding the facts. The church destroyed so thoroughly all writings about him and his work, that there is much the world will never know about him and his work, especially during that part of his life when he was most active.

In the book titled *Life of Apollonius* by Philostratus, there is a gap that covers nearly the whole of what was called the period of the teachings of Jesus, which the apostles later continued.

Had the Memories of the *Life of Apollonius* by Barnabas, also known as Damis, and the *Biography of Apollonius* by Philostratus, been permitted to come down to us as written, there would be no Jesus today and not a vestige of Christianity would be in existence.

Chapter No. 12
Philosophy of Nature

"There can be no priesthood where Life is understood, hence the obscurantism (in the Bible). To this (concealment relative to Life) is due much of the race's ignorance today. It served the benighted Arian and Piscean Ages, but it will not do for the Aquarian. The race forever living by a delusion (*Quartum Organum,* 1959, by Krypton, page, 491).

The Superstitious Heathens, as the Mother Church calls the Ancient Pagans, had a Philosophy of Life, but no fraudulent religion and no anthropomorphic God. These were invented by the priesthood to give them a job to look after this God's business, because he was not able to do it himself. He had done it for millions of years, and then scheming man decided he needed their help.

History informs us that the Masters of Atlantis carried to Egypt their Fire Philosophy of Life, and Doctor R.S. Clymer said:

"It gave to its votaries definite knowledge of the actual Fire within their own souls, being that power which characterizes those who have raised themselves to a level about that of the earthly-minded" (page 180).

Marie Corelli, one of the most famous of modern authors, in her book, *"A Romance of Two Worlds"* made this statement:

"Yours? What? That which you call your own? Listen, every talent you have, every breath you draw, every drop of blood flowing in your body, is lent to you, and you must pay it all back."

We want the reader to remember that in this present work there is nothing new, nor is it ours. We examine and analyze the works of others who have labored in their special field before us; have endeavored to select there from such material as deals with the special subject, and arranged it to form a philosophical treatise on the Arcanum of Creation.

Modern science does not understand the deeper secrets of Creation, but the Ancient Magi did, and they have handed the knowledge down in one form or another from Initiate to Initiate. Usually they were taught in the Secret Schools established for that purpose, and, more often, taught privately and in certain places little suspected as being seats of learning or caves of knowledge, maintained secretly by an Ancient Brotherhood of the August Fraternity.

History informs us that when man recognized the relation existing between himself and all other created objects in the world, he realized that he was only a part of the whole, and subject to all the laws which governed the whole.

The bugs and the birds have no sickness, no doctors, no drugs, no hospitals, and yet they are ruled by the same law that governs man. What makes such a great difference? They are guided by *Cosmic Consciousness* as we have expounded in our work of that title. But man was released from that control by the endowment of Free Will, to permit him to rise to a higher level, and he went the other way, due to the clever work of those who live and thrive on human misery.

In our work published in 1926, titled *"Law of Life & Human Health"*, (available at www.frontlinebookpublishing.com) we referred to certain functions of the body, not understood by medical science, which reveal the marvelous work of Creation. We showed that in all cases of common sickness man should observe the laws of Creation with poisons fraudulently called medicine. There is no medicine.

The body can never, under any circumstances, use beneficially anything made by man, who cannot make a blade of grass nor a grain of corn, and knows so little about the processes of the body that he cannot make a drop of blood nor expound how the body makes it.

Medical science claims the blood is made of what man eats. We have shown in our work titled *"The Empyreal Sea"* (available at www.frontlinebookpublishing.com) that such is not the case. The blood and the life of the body are not the products of what man eats and drinks. The body would have to be alive before it needed food and drink. This means the blood was flowing thru the body before food and drink were taken.

As proof of the certainty of this assertion, deprive man briefly of the electrified radiation which enters his lungs with every breath he takes, and he expires quickly, gasping for the *Breath of Life* like a helpless fish lifted from the silvery stream.

Man and all created objects of the living kingdom are not constituted of nor sustained by "used" material. Food is a "second-hand" substance, and that "used" substance is never employed by Creation in any of its work. Creation always uses fresh material in all its work, directly from the cosmic reservoir. And that substance is Electrified Radiation

The first form of philosophical inculcation of which we have any record was that derived from Atlantis, and known as the Hermetic Philosophy. The next was a modified form thereof, and appeared in the Mysteries of Osiris and Isis in Egypt. Osiris represented the Sun and Isis represented Mother Earth.

These teachings were taken from Hermetic Philosophy, but went on further, in that they included the mystery involved in both Generation and Regeneration — those mysteries based on the Divinity of Sex in its dual manifestation, as we expounded forty years ago in our great work titled *"Secret of Regeneration."* (available at www.frontlinebookpublishing.com)

The Ancient Mysteries was the great institution of the Philosophy of Life in the Pagan World, and that was the school which Constantine the Great was determined to crush when he established Christianity in the 4th Century. Branches of that institution existed in all leading countries of the ancient world, and the chief Principles involved represented the Glorious Sun and Mother Earth. In Egypt these were symbolized as Osiris and Isis.

The Ancient Mysteries presented a singular unity of design, clearly indicating a common origin and a purity of doctrine as evidently proving that this origin was not to be sought for in the popular theology of the Pagan world.

These mysteries owed their origin to the desire of the Ancient Magi to establish esoteric philosophy, in which would be concealed from the popular approach those sublime facts of Creation which it was considered could be entrusted only to those who had previously been prepared for their reception.

By the confinement of this philosophy to a system of secret knowledge, guarded by the most rigid rites, could it be protected from unscrupulous groups that would corrupt and propagate it for their profit and Power?

In referring to this phase of the question, Oliver wrote:

"The distinguished few who retained their fidelity, uncontaminated by the contagion of evil example, would soon be able to estimate the superior benefits of an isolated and protected institution, which afforded the advantage of a select society, and kept at a distance the profane scoffer, whose presence might pollute their pure devotion and social converse, by contumelious language and unholy mirth."

And the prevention of this intrusion and the preservation of these sublime truths, was the original object of the institution of the ceremonies of initiation, and the adoption of other means by which the initiated could be recognized and the uninitiated excluded.

In speaking of the Mysteries, Dollinger said:

"The whole was arranged as a drama, the prelude to which consisted in purifications, sacrifices of personal desires, and injunctions with regard to the behavior to be observed. The adventures of certain symbolical deities, their suffering and joys, their appearance on earth, and relations to mankind, their death, or descent to the nether world, their return, or their rising again — all these, as symbolizing the life of Nature, were represented in a connected series of dramatical scenes.

And behold what Christianity did with this ancient Philosophy of Life of the Pagan World.

Professor E.G. Barrett said: "When we attempt to analyze the Christian Religion as it is today, and as it has been for a thousand years, we find it impossible to separate truth from error, or to unravel a most baffling mess.

"We find that this religious system is a synthetic one, with no real background of its own. It is built up out of borrowed and stolen ideas and beliefs, 'lifted' from every possible source."

Perhaps the most amazing feature of the whole proposition is the fraudulent manner in which the "pious church fathers" made their "Holy Bible," and the gullibility of the deceived masses in swallowing the fraud as "the Word of God."

1967: Once again this famous author has given to the world a new and unusual manuscript. Those who mourn the dead will be most interested in this work. *The Golden Dawn,* sharply gleaming on the distant horizon, denotes the approach of a brighter day in the life of man, the Lord of the whole earth *(Zachariah 4:14)*. The millions of innocent people, sustained by the fear of death, sees the brilliant sign and shudders. For the sign heralds the revival of knowledge that will inform man of the mysteries of creation and liberate his mind from the fear of death. Man will learn that he is life, and that life had no beginning and has no ending. What appears as death pertains only to the body and not to life. The body was never alive. It was only the mechanism used by life to perform certain work of Creation in the visible world.

Ancient Secret of Personal Power:
Tetragrammation

Good Health is the very foundation of Success. And we have heard health is man's birthright. That is another grievous error. Good health is the reward received by him who earns it. Contents: *Kingdom within, Perfection is within, Secrets of the Body, Mysterious Glands, Seven Astral Centers, Tetragrammation, Science of Sensology, Edocrinology, Higher Consciousness, Theology, Seership, Astral Light, Living Fire, Macrocosm, Time-Eternity.*

Ancient Sun God

Contents: *The Ancient Light, The Great Sun God, Secret of the Stars, Astrology Changed to Astronomy, Virgin Mother, Majesty of God's Kingdom, The Sovereign Sun, Ab-Ram the Sun-God, Lamb of God, Perfection.*

Awaken the World Within

Contents: The Course of Study, 58 wonderful lessons. *These lessons show how the higher faculties of mind and soul may be aroused and activated, thus enabling the body, through which the real man contacts the physical plane, to express the noblest characteristics. If you are seeking the highest spheres of mental, physical existence, you should find in these lessons the help and guidance you need.*

Cosmic Science of the Ancient Masters

Contents: *If a man die, shall he live again? Is reincarnation a fact? The sublime truths of the Universe. The Mysteries of Nature, of Man; The Grand Cycle of Creation, Conscious & Subconscious Mind, Intuition, Immorality, Dormant Organs, The Mysterious Chambers in the Skull.* Highly Illustrated with rare Occult Illustrations.

The Kingdom of Heaven

Contents: *The Grand Cosmic Kingdom and its Seven Parts. The Mental Kingdom; Consciousness and Super-consciousness; Why People Fail; Freedom and Slavery; The Spiritual Organs and Powers; The State of Brahma; Telepathy and Television; The Fourth Dimension.*

Living Fire or God's Law of Life

Contents: *The Ageless Wisdom of the Ancient masters tells us that the Divine Trinity is reflected in man, and his Knowledge, when correctly and clearly interpreted as Hotema has presented it in his various works, will lift the veil that darkens the Mind and reveal to the understanding of man the facts of Eternal Life.*

The Magic Wand

Contents: *The Serpentine Fire, its energizing through the subtle body centers (chakras): Mastery over the senses; Awakening of the 6th and 7th senses; The Black and White Serpent; The Golden Oil of Kanda; Biblical truths that have been Suppressed.*

The Magic World

Hotema tells a private story about himself that he has never before told in his writings. Contents: *Magic Intelligence, Magic World, Magic Esotericism, Magic and Mystery, Magic Creation, Magic Message, Magic Spirit, Magic Kingdom, Magic Wires, Magic Sensology, Magic Chambers, The Magician, Magic Light, Magic Attraction, Magic Mate, Magic Practice, Magic End.*

Man's Higher Consciousness

Contents: *The author claims this work shows the reason why the radio and television mechanism in the human skull fails to respond fully now to cosmic radiation as it did twenty thousand years ago, when the Ancient Masters accumulated their wisdom of Creation, Life and Man, then recorded it in fable and fiction, for interpretation to those who proved by test they were worthy to receive the same. The author covers subjects such as daily exercise, vegetarian diet, raw foods, sunbathing, periodical fasting, deep breathing, history of longevity, cosmic forces, secrets of the ancient masters.*

The Mysterious Sphinx

Contents: *Why is it an object of awe and reverence. A startling expose showing how a symbol for the ancient masters evolved into the God of Christianity. The secret of the Cosmic Principles which Constitute Man; The Lost Word; The Vital Principle of Life; How the Masters Communed with the Cosmic Powers and Principle; How symbolism Develops Man.*

The Magic Temple (Forthcoming Spring 2019)

Contents: *The amazing powers of the human body. The author says the world is still trying to solve the mystery of man. Is God as described in the first book of the bible? The evolutionists refuse to consider that fabulous account, and assert that man is the product of creation. People grow up in that confusion and know not what to believe. There is no death, as religion teaches. Food does not build blood as science teaches. Food doesn't give nourishment to the body as taught by the dietitians. Man need not die at 100 years. He quotes scores of unusual facts seldom found in the average textbook.*

The Mystery of Man

Contents: *The cosmic process of transforming solarized man into physical man, Illusions, The dual aspect, The identity of ego, The secret of the atom, Doctrine of numbers.*

The Facts of Nutrition

Contents: *The variety of the organism depends not on the food and drink, for experience teaches athletes to go into action with empty stomachs. The author gives his concepts that the growth of the body does not result from food consumption, but from the division and subdivision of the parent cell. What food does not and cannot produce, it cannot and does not sustain.*

The Genesis of Christianity

Contents: *Hilton Hotema started in Sunday School — he went regularly until he was fifteen. At twelve, he began the study of the Bible in earnest. He became a preacher and after preaching in scores of different states and finally found the truth was not being given to the people. He began comparing the various Bible and religious books and found many startling facts which were never given to the people from the pulpit ... never taught in public schools, nor in Sunday Schools. He found the average preacher knew a little about the history of the bible, and was shouting about things that were not true. He discovered why the Roman Empire was plunged into mental darkness with the birth of Christianity. That darkness was necessary to help the priesthood frighten people, to keep the priesthood in high places, and to drive the multitude into the church, for the sake of profit and power. He shows why Moses could not have written the Pentateuch (The first five books of the Bible — the account of his own demise — Deuteronomy 3)*

The Glorious Resurrection (Forthcoming Spring 2019)

Contents: *Symbolism; Ancient Science; Crucified Saviors; Great Mother of the Gods; Mysterious Resurrection; Birth of Gods; Light; Two Bodies in One; Ancient Terminology; Mystic Sleep; Life Swindle of Mytheography; Unknown Joy of Death; The Future Life; Reincarnation; The Universal Fable.*

The Golden Dawn

Contents: *Those who mourn the dead will be most interested in this work. The Golden Dawn, sharply gleaming on the distant horizon, denotes the approach of a brighter day in the life of man, the Lord of the whole world earth (Zechariah 4:14). The millions of innocent people, sustained by fear of death, sees the brilliant signs and shudders. For the sign heralds the revival of knowledge that will inform man of the mysteries of creation and liberate his mind from fear of death. Man will learn that he is life, and that life has no beginning and has no ending. What appears as death pertains only to the body and not to life. The body was never alive. It was only the mechanism used by life to perform certain work of creation in the visible world.*

The Great Law

Contents: *Professor Hotema studied the teachings of the Ancients from hidden and revealed sources for over seventy years. He was a student of many movements and teachings, Rosicrucian, Theosophy, Hindu, Hebrew, Egyptian and Grecian Mysteries, Magian Tradition, Masonry, the Tarot, Arcane Sciences, Hygiene, Vegetarian, and many others of which the* world has never heard. He delved into ancient records and gathered scattered and widely separated fragments of truth from the ruins of temples of the Masters who were so far ahead of us in knowledge and wisdom that only the few can interpret their true meaning. And he has interpreted it, boiled it down, condensed it into readily comprehensible material.

The Great Red Dragon

Contents: *Ancient Scriptures, Tree of Life, Thou Shalt Surely Die, Act of Propagation, Coition and Convulsions, Pituitary Tumors, Sin Unto Death, Card 6 Temptation, Woman Appears first, the Degenerate Woman, Man a Degenerate woman, analysis of Homosexuality.*

The Secret of Regeneration (Book I)

Contents: Some of the 128 Chapters — *Truth, The Dark Ages, Age of Ignorance, Age of the Earth, Age of Man, Sunken Continents, The Antediluvian World, Ancient Cultures, People of Atlantis, Despots and Tyrants, Nineveh and Assyria, The Chaldeans, The Hebrews, Israelites in Egypt, Driven out of Egypt, The Babylonian Captivity, The Scriptures of the Jews, The First Forgery, The Priest and the Scribe, The Second Forgery, The Pentateuch, The Third Forgery, Story of the Exodus, Biblical Contradictions, The Fourth Forgery, The Synoptic Gospels, Many Gospels, The Work of the Priesthood, The Need for Gospels, The Essenes, Pious Fraud, Ecclesiastical Lying and Forgery, Argument Against Christianity, Is Jesus a Myth/ Deceiving the Masses, How the Church Triumphed, etc., etc., etc.*

The Secret of Regeneration (Book II)

Contents: Some of the 84 Chapters — *Sex Symbols, The Garden of Eden, The Tree of Knowledge, The Serpent, The Sons of God, The Law of Nature, Evolution vs. Devolution, Law of Cause and Effect, The Perfect Man, Degeneration of the Gods, Sex and Seed, Similitude of the Sexes, Rudimentary Organs, Appearance of Woman, Law of Variation, The Hermaphrodite, Amativeness, Sexual Consciousness, Asexuality, Auto-Sexuality, Degradation of Women, Sex in Religion, Morality & the Church, Woman under Church Rule, Traces of Woman Rule, Marriage, Woman the Superior, Is Coition Natural for Men, Coition & Convulsions, The Virgin Mother, Preventing Impregnation Mentally, Fornication & Imagination, Woman Appears First, The Degenerate Woman, Man a Degenerate Woman, Perfect Man Born, Not Made.*

The Divine Life

Contents: *What is Life, Dust of the Ground, Breath of Life, Law of Creation, Law of Change, Creative Force, Origin of Life, Kinds of Life, Hidden Artist, Man is Not Life, When Man Begins to Live, Relation of Man to Life, Man Does Nothing of Himself, Influence of Tradition, Ancient Worship Rules Today, In Spirit and in Truth, What is the Soul? The Mysterious Force, What is Intuition, Voice of the Soul, Divine Intelligence, Why Men are Mocked, Death Penalty of Disobedience, The Great Commandment, How Long Should Man Live? Fountain of Youth, Human Intellect, Was Man Born to Die, Influence of Suggestion, Conditions of Eternal Life, How old is the Body, From Master to Slave, Where is Hell? Where is Heaven? Doctrine of Atonement,*

Return to Obedience, Life Eternal, Dust Returns to the Ground, Spirit Returns to the Creator, Life Eternal, World of the Dead.

Live Longer

Contents: *Right Living, Healthful Environment, Climate, Man's Home, The Artificial World, The Art of Living, He Lived 370 Years, Law of Change, Fountain of Youth, Man Once Lived 80,000 Years, Self-Denial.*

Empyreal Sea: How High Do You Climb: Live 1,400 Years

Contents: *The Human Temple, Man Created Perfect, The Aging Process, Secret of Living, The River of Life, The River of Death, Breathing, Eating, Food the Killer, Living Without Eating, Law of Adaption, What is the Empyreal Sea? Search for Longevity, The Perfect Organization, Man's Place in Creation, The Creative Power, The Divine Curse, Marriage, The New Age, Procreation and Expiration, Degeneration.*

More Praise For Professor Hilton Hotema

"Your writings have entirely changed my course of thought and so enriched my life that I am eager to read everything you have written and in my consciousness there is a deep sense of gratitude toward you."

— E. Los <u>Angeles, California.</u>

"I have been reading books on Health and Philosophy for more than 40 years. "May I say that the books written by Professor Hilton Hotema, which I recently purchased from you, are by far the most instructive and the most original I have ever read. I am at a loss for words to give adequate praise to Professor Hotema. Assuring you of my great satisfaction and wishing your company a well-deserved success.

— I remain, <u>L. G. T. Coronado, California."</u>

"I want to express my complete satisfaction for Professor Hilton Hotema's writings, as I find his books very stimulating and educational for sound thinking. Please add the additional books I have selected".

— <u>Thomas Mazucci,</u> New York.

"My wife and I have completed your Hotema Folio (12 books), for the second time. If I could be granted one wish for the greater good for the human race it would be, that every man and woman should read this folio at least once. We have been members of the Rosicrucian Order for many years, and the lessons and instructions covered many of the things in the folio, and prepared our minds for a better understanding."

— George O. Keefer, Los Alamos, New Mexico.

"I have just finished reading *"Man's Higher Consciousness,"* by Professor Hilton Hotema. I think it is a most wonderful book. I think it is the whole truth. I wish I had the information it contains earlier in my life. Many thanks to Professor Hilton Hotema.

— Edmund Groben, Indiana.

"These books have forced me to revise, somewhat reluctantly, of course, a good many of my former 'College degree' ideas about the whole subject of Health. This I am glad to do because now, for the first time I have a clear picture framed in my mind of both the 'beginning and the end' — as it were of what it means to attempt true healing in patients. I would insistently recommend these books to everyone interested in knowing the true facts, especially those whose mission it is to help an ailing Humanity".

— Doctor Amil H. Sprehn, Member International Society of Naturopathic Physicians.

www.ingramcontent.com/pod-product-compliance
Lightning Source LLC
Chambersburg PA
CBHW050551280326
41933CB00011B/1801